Organizational Behavior - Negative Aspects

Edited by Kivanc Bozkus

Published in London, United Kingdom

Organizational Behavior - Negative Aspects
http://dx.doi.org/10.5772/intechopen.1000251
Edited by Kivanc Bozkus

Contributors
Kivanc Bozkus, Semra Köse, Olga Lainidi, Vilma Chalili, Ilias Maliousis, Maria Spiliou, Eva Tzioti, Panagiota Koutsimani, Anthony Montgomery, Ugwu Callistus Chinwuba, Mary Clare Coghlan, Andrew B. Ross, Mia B. Russell, Tom Karp, Belal Panahi, Huijeong Oh

First published in London, United Kingdom, 2023 by IntechOpen
IntechOpen is the global imprint of INTECHOPEN LIMITED, registered in England and Wales, registration number: 11086078, 5 Princes Gate Court, London, SW7 2QJ, United Kingdom

British Library Cataloguing-in-Publication Data
A catalogue record for this book is available from the British Library

Additional hard and PDF copies can be obtained from orders@intechopen.com

Organizational Behavior - Negative Aspects
Edited by Kivanc Bozkus
p. cm.
Print ISBN 978-1-83769-574-4
Online ISBN 978-1-83769-573-7
eBook (PDF) ISBN 978-1-83769-575-1

Meet the editor

Dr. Bozkus is an associate professor at Artvin Coruh University, Turkey. He obtained a bachelor's degree in Science Teaching and worked as a science teacher. He received a graduate education grant from the Ministry of National Education and a master's degree in Educational Leadership from Penn State University, USA. He obtained a Ph.D. in Educational Administration from Anadolu University, Turkey. His research interests are the professional development of teachers, school development, leadership, and organizational behavior.

Contents

Preface

Organizational Behavior – Negative Aspects delves into the intricate world of organizational behavior, shedding light on the often-overlooked negative aspects that can impact individuals, teams, and entire organizations. By exploring these darker dimensions, we aim to foster a deeper understanding of the challenges organizations face and provide insights for addressing them.

The journey into the negative aspects of organizational behavior begins with my introductory chapter, which sets the stage by providing an overview of the topic and highlighting the importance of exploring the darker side of organizational behavior.

In Chapter 2, "The Dark Side of Organizational Behavior", Semra Köse uncovers the less desirable aspects that can arise within the organizational context.

Chapter 3, "Perspective Chapter: The Dark Triad in the Organization – A Review of the Evidence and Future Recommendations", by Olga Lainidi, Vilma Chalili, Ilias Maliousis, Maria Spiliou, Eva Tzioti, Panagiota Koutsimani, and Anthony Montgomery reviews the evidence surrounding the concept of the "Dark Triad" and provides future recommendations for understanding and addressing its implications.

In Chapter 4, "Counterproductive Workplace Behaviors (CWBs): Antecedents and Outcomes", Ugwu Callistus Chinwuba explores the causes and consequences of counterproductive workplace behaviors and highlights the importance of mitigating their impact.

In Chapter 5, "Why Fear Crushes Your Culture", Mary Clare Coghlan, Andrew B. Ross and Mia B. Russell bring our attention to the detrimental effects of fear on organizational culture. This thought-provoking chapter uncovers the detrimental effects of fear and provides insights for cultivating a healthier work environment.

Chapter 6, "Perspective Chapter: We expect Effective Leadership from Leaders, but is this the Case in Reality? Reframing a Much-Hyped Phenomenon by Investigating the Antithesis" by Tom Karp, presents a perspective on leadership. By investigating the antithesis, this chapter challenges conventional notions of effective leadership, urging readers to reconsider their expectations.

Belal Panahi explores the impact of technology on individuals and organizations in Chapter 7, "Techno-Stress in Organization". By examining the stressors arising from the integration of technology, this chapter highlights the need for effective management strategies in the digital age.

Finally, in Chapter 8, "Negative Aspects of Teacher Burnout Problem on Educational Organization", Huijeong Oh sheds light on the profound impact of teacher burnout on educational institutions, emphasizing the importance of addressing this issue for the well-being of both teachers and students.

Together, these chapters provide a comprehensive exploration of the negative aspects of organizational behavior, offering valuable insights for researchers, practitioners, and individuals interested in understanding and addressing these challenges.

I would like to extend my heartfelt gratitude to all the authors and specifically acknowledge Author Service Manager Zrinka Tomicic at IntechOpen, whose invaluable contributions greatly enhanced the editorial process.

I hope that this edited volume serves as a catalyst for further research and dialogue on the negative aspects of organizational behavior. May it inspire new perspectives, strategies, and interventions that contribute to healthier and more productive organizations.

Kivanc Bozkus
Artvin Coruh University,
Artvin, Turkey

Chapter 1

Introductory Chapter: Exploring the Negative Aspects of Organizational Behavior

Kivanc Bozkus

1. Introduction

Organizational behavior is the study of how individuals and groups interact within an organization, and how these interactions affect the performance and effectiveness of the organization. While the study of organizational behavior has produced many insights into how organizations can function more effectively, there are also negative aspects of organizational behavior that can have a significant impact on organizational performance. The negative side of organizational behavior refers to the adverse effects that certain organizational behaviors can have on individuals, groups, and the organization. This negative side is often overlooked or downplayed, but it can have significant consequences for the health and well-being of employees, the overall functioning of the organization, and its bottom line. Overall, the negative side of organizational behavior is a significant concern for organizations and their employees. Understanding the causes and consequences of these negative behaviors is essential for creating a safe, healthy, and productive work environment. In this introductory chapter, I will explore the negative side of organizational behavior, with a focus on conflict, dysfunctional leadership, unethical behavior, workplace stress, workplace bullying, mobbing, and dark traits of personality.

2. Conflict

Conflict between individuals and groups within the organization has the potential to be one of the most detrimental features of organizational behavior. Differences in values or ideas, rivalry for resources or power, or personal enmity are just a few causes of conflict that might occur. Conflict may have a big impact on how well a company performs because it can hinder teamwork and communication as well as undermine employee trust and motivation. Conflict can have a big impact on how well an organization performs, according to research. For instance, research [1] revealed that disagreement might hinder innovation and creativity within firms because staff members may be less likely to share ideas and work together when they believe that their opinions are not appreciated or valued. Similar findings were made by another study [2], which indicated that conflict might decrease trust and increase employee turnover because people may be less motivated to work with somebody they do not trust.

3. Dysfunctional leadership

Leadership dysfunction is yet another detrimental component of corporate behavior. Leadership that is ineffective, unethical, or destructive to the organization or its members is referred to as dysfunctional leadership. Micromanagement, bullying, and abusive conduct are a few manifestations of dysfunctional leadership. Organizational performance can be significantly impacted by dysfunctional leadership since it can result in lower staff morale, more employee turnover, and diminished employee trust. For instance, a study [3] discovered that aggressive leadership might result in lower work satisfaction and higher staff turnover. Similar findings were made by another study [4], which discovered that managers who engage in bullying behavior can decrease organizational engagement and raise employee turnover intentions.

4. Unethical behavior

Another unfavorable feature of organizational behavior that can have a major effect on performance is unethical behavior. Dishonest, illegal, or destructive activity is referred to as unethical behavior. Fraud, theft, and harassment are a few instances of unethical behavior. Because it can result in legal responsibility, harm to the organization's brand, and a decline in employee and customer trust, unethical behavior can have a big impact on how well an organization performs. For instance, a study [5] discovered that unethical behavior can cause a decline in company engagement and an increase in employee turnover intentions. Similarly, another study [6] indicated that unethical behavior by leaders might lead to poor job satisfaction and greater turnover intentions among employees.

5. Workplace stress

Workplace stress is a typical organizational behavior flaw that lowers productivity and increases attrition, absenteeism, and burnout. It is described as a physical and psychological reaction to job expectations that are more than one's capacity for coping [7]. Heavy workloads [8], role ambiguity [9], bad relationships with coworkers and managers, and organizational change [10] are all factors that contribute to workplace stress. Reduced productivity, lower-quality work [11], more absenteeism [12], turnover [13], and burnout [14] are some repercussions of workplace stress. Burnout causes a decline in motivation, job satisfaction, and absenteeism [15]. Offering tools like counseling services, stress management classes, and flexible work schedules is one way to manage workplace stress [7]. Another tactic is to foster a healthy work atmosphere by promoting sociability, allowing opportunities for professional development, and giving feedback and appreciation [16]. Organizations can resolve role ambiguity by giving clear job descriptions, goals, and regular feedback while also reducing workload stress by setting realistic deadlines, offering support, and encouraging breaks [8].

6. Workplace bullying

Workplace bullying, which is defined as persistent destructive behavior aimed at certain people or groups, is a serious problem in organizational behavior [17]. It can appear in a variety of ways, including sabotage, social exclusion, and verbal abuse. Bullying at work has serious detrimental effects on employee morale, attrition rates, and overall health, including stress, despair, and anxiety [18]. Individual qualities, corporate culture, and power dynamics are all factors that might contribute to bullying in the workplace [17]. Age, gender, and low self-esteem are characteristics that make people more susceptible to bullying [17, 18]. Bullying is encouraged by toxic workplace situations that accept hostility, whereas it is discouraged by organizations that emphasize respect and collaboration [17]. Bullies who abuse their position of power or influence also have a role [17]. Bullying at work has an effect on both individuals and businesses. Victims frequently exhibit increased absenteeism due to the detrimental impacts on their health, performance, and job satisfaction [17]. High turnover rates harm an organization's ability to recruit, train, and produce workers [18]. A bullying culture in the workplace also breeds mistrust, distrust, and reputational damage [18], as well as negative effects on the law and finances [17]. Organizations should implement strategies like transparent policies, manager and employee training, fostering positive work environments, encouraging reporting, and promptly dealing with incidents through investigations, victim support, and disciplinary actions [17] to prevent and address workplace bullying.

7. Mobbing

When a group attacks a person and causes psychological injury, it is called mobbing [19]. It comprises physical intimidation, verbal assault, slander, and social exclusion. Mobbing is severe and pervasive, with numerous incidents of harassment occurring over time and being planned by a group [20, 21]. Mobbing has a profound impact on victims. They could go through PTSD, depression, and anxiety [17]. There may also be physical complaints, such as headaches and sleeplessness [20]. The psychological effects can result in poor performance, decreased job satisfaction, and trouble finding new employment [17]. Social support may dwindle, which might cause feelings of loneliness [17]. Individual, organizational, and societal variables all play a role in mobbing. Aggression, low self-esteem, and a drive for control are all personal issues [19]. Along with high job demands, little job management, and inadequate leadership, organizational culture, and societal views also have a role [17, 20]. Individualism and competition can encourage mobbing [19]. Intervention and prevention must be prioritized. Building a cooperative and respectful organizational culture is an important component of prevention [21]. Investigations, clear reporting procedures, and training are crucial. Intervention tackles workplace pressures, enhances leadership and management, and addresses core causes [17]. Mobbing victims should receive support, such as counseling and legal representation.

8. Dark traits of personality

Positive and negative personality qualities can be separated into categories. The "dark traits of personality," or unfavorable characteristics, include psychopathy, narcissism, Machiavellianism, and sadism [22, 23]. These characteristics have an impact on organizational behavior and have an impact on employee well-being, leadership, and job performance. The Dark Tetrad includes sadism, while the Dark Triad consists of psychopathy, narcissism, and Machiavellianism [22, 23]. Each feature has distinct manifestations, such as grandiosity and entitlement for narcissism [24], and fearlessness, impulsivity, and meanness for psychopathy [25]. In contrast to sadism, which emphasizes hostility and cruelty toward others, Machiavellianism combines strategic manipulation and a pessimistic outlook [26]. Although dark characteristics are frequently researched separately, they frequently co-occur in people [27]. Dark characteristics can impact work performance in both positive and negative ways. Psychopathy may encourage more inventiveness and risk-taking, while narcissism may increase self-assurance and boldness [28, 29]. However, negative qualities can also result in unethical behavior, unproductive work habits, and aggressive interpersonal behavior [23, 26].

Author details

Kivanc Bozkus
Artvin Coruh University, Artvin, Turkey

*Address all correspondence to: kbozkus@artvin.edu.tr

References

[1] De Dreu CK, Weingart L. Task versus relationship conflict, team performance, and team member satisfaction: A meta-analysis. Journal of Applied Psychology. 2003;**88**(4):741-749. DOI: 10.1037/0021-9010.88.4.741

[2] Jehn KA, Bezrukova K. A field study of group diversity, workgroup context, and performance. Journal of Organizational Behavior. 2004;**25**(6):703-729. DOI: 10.1002/job.258

[3] Schyns B, Schilling J. How bad are the effects of bad leaders? A meta-analysis of destructive leadership and its outcomes. The Leadership Quarterly. 2013;**24**(1):138-158. DOI: 10.1016/j.leaqua.2012.09.001

[4] Tepper BJ, Moss SE, Duffy MK. Predictors of abusive supervision: Supervisor perceptions of deep-level dissimilarity, relationship conflict, and subordinate performance. Academy of Management Journal. 2011;**54**(2):279-294. DOI: 10.5465/amj.2011.60263084

[5] Treviño LK, Weaver GR, Reynolds SJ. Behavioral ethics in organizations: A review. Journal of Management. 2006;**32**(6):951-990. DOI: 10.1177/0149206306294258

[6] Zhu W, Treviño LK, Zheng X. Ethical leadership and follower voice and performance: The role of follower identifications and entity morality beliefs. The Leadership Quarterly. 2016;**27**(5):728-744. DOI: 10.1016/j.leaqua.2016.02.004

[7] Houdmont J, Leka S. An Introduction to Occupational Health Psychology. Hoboken, NJ: Wiley-Blackwell; 2010

[8] Nahrgang JD, Morgeson FP, Hofmann DA. Safety at work: A meta-analytic investigation of the link between job demands, job resources, burnout, engagement, and safety outcomes. Journal of Applied Psychology. 2011;**96**(1):71-94

[9] Kahn RL, Wolfe DM, Quinn RP, Snoek JD, Rosenthal RA. Organizational Stress: Studies in Role Conflict and Ambiguity. Hoboken, NJ: John Wiley & Sons; 1964

[10] Cameron KS, Green M. Making Sense of Change Management: A Complete Guide to the Models, Tools and Techniques of Organizational Change. London: Kogan Page Publishers; 2015

[11] Sonnentag S, Frese M. Stress in organizations. Handbook of Psychology, Industrial and Organizational Psychology. 2012;**3**:560-592

[12] Grosch JW, Caruso CC, Rosa RR, Sauter SL, Schill AL. Long hours of work in the US: Associations with demographic and organizational characteristics, psychosocial working conditions, and health. American Journal of Industrial Medicine. 2006;**49**(11):943-952

[13] Bridger RS, Day DV. Decomposing daily job satisfaction and its relationship with quit intentions and actual turnover. Journal of Occupational and Organizational Psychology. 2011;**84**(1):113-127

[14] Maslach C, Leiter MP. Understanding the burnout experience: Recent research and its implications for psychiatry. World Psychiatry. 2016;**15**(2):103-111

[15] Schaufeli WB, Enzmann D. The Burnout Companion to Study and Practice: A Critical Analysis. Philadelphia, PA: CRC Press; 1998

[16] Kelloway EK, Hurrell JJ Jr, Day A. Workplace interventions for occupational stress. In: Näswall K, Hellgren J, Sverke M, editors. The Individual in the Changing Working Life. Cambridge: Cambridge University Press; 2008. pp. 419-441

[17] Einarsen S, Hoel H, Zapf D, Cooper CL. The concept of bullying and harassment at work: The European tradition. In: Bullying and Harassment in the Workplace: Developments in Theory, Research, and Practice. Philadelphia, PA: CRC Press; 2011. pp. 3-39

[18] Hauge LJ, Skogstad A, Einarsen S. The relative impact of workplace bullying as a social stressor at work. Scandinavian Journal of Psychology. 2010;**51**(5):426-433

[19] Namie G, Namie R. The Bully at Work: What you Can Do to Stop the Hurt and Reclaim your Dignity on the Job. Naperville, IL: Sourcebooks, Inc.; 2003

[20] Lutgen-Sandvik P. Take this job and...: Quitting and other forms of resistance to workplace bullying. Communication Monographs. 2006;**73**(4):406-433

[21] Zapf D, Einarsen S, Vartia M, Empereur JL. Escalated harassment in the workplace: Individual, organizational, and societal causes. In: Einarsen S, Hoel H, Zapf D, Cooper CL, editors. Bullying and Harassment in the Workplace: Developments in Theory, Research, and Practice. London: Taylor & Francis; 2011. pp. 249-272

[22] Paulhus DL, Williams KM. The dark triad of personality: Narcissism, Machiavellianism, and psychopathy. Journal of Research in Personality. 2002;**36**(6):556-563

[23] Buckels EE, Jones DN, Paulhus DL. Behavioral confirmation of everyday sadism. Psychological Science. 2013;**24**(11):2201-2209

[24] Miller JD, McCain J, Lynam DR, Few LR, Gentile B, MacKillop J, et al. A comparison of the criterion validity of popular measures of narcissism and narcissistic personality disorder via the use of expert ratings. Psychological Assessment. 2014;**26**(3):958

[25] Skeem JL, Polaschek DL, Patrick CJ, Lilienfeld SO. Psychopathic personality: Bridging the gap between scientific evidence and public policy. Psychological Science in the Public Interest. 2011;**12**(3):95-162

[26] Jones DN, Paulhus DL. Machiavellianism. In: Leary MR, Hoyle RH, editors. Handbook of Individual Differences in Social Behavior. New York: Guilford Press; 2009. pp. 93-108

[27] Furnham A, Richards SC, Paulhus DL. The dark triad of personality: A 10-year review. Social and Personality Psychology Compass. 2013;**7**(3):199-216

[28] Nevicka B, Ten Velden FS, De Hoogh AHB, Van Vianen AEM. Reality at odds with perceptions: Narcissistic leaders and group performance. Psychological Science. 2011;**22**:1259-1264. DOI: 10.1177/0956797611417259

[29] O'Boyle EH Jr, Forsyth DR, Banks GC, McDaniel MA. A meta-analysis of the dark triad and work behavior: A social exchange perspective. Journal of Applied Psychology. 2012;**97**(3):557-579

Chapter 2

The Dark Side of Organizational Behavior

Semra Köse

Abstract

In the literature of management and organization studies, the emphasis on the importance of human capital has increased with Neoclassical and later Modern management approaches after the Classical Period. The emphasis on the importance of human capital and human factor has increased with Neoclassical and later Modern management approaches after the Classical Period. With the understanding that the most important resource that organizations have is human, all kinds of positive and negative behaviors that the members of the organization will display in their workplaces appear as an important element for the business to continue its activities and gain competitive advantage. At this point, traditional organization and organizational behavior theories are shaped within the framework of rational human behavior. However, it is an undeniable fact that the behaviors exhibited by human nature will not always be positive and that negative attitudes will affect organizations and other individuals in different areas. Positivist organizational approaches, which deal with the behavior of organizational members in the context of cause-effect relationships, generally focus on the positive behaviors of employees. The dark side of organizational behavior, which is a reflection of irrational human behaviors and harms businesses with its negative consequences, has become one of the important research areas in recent years. It is important to determine how the irrational human factor, which traditional organizational behavior theories lack, can be directed in line with organizational goals. At this point, the necessity of considering all kinds of positive and negative behaviors exhibited by individuals with a holistic perspective emerges. The negative attitudes and behaviors in question represent the dark side of the organizational field. In this study, in which some basic concepts that make up the dark side of organizations are discussed, the antecedents, reasons, and reflections of the aforementioned behaviors in the organizational field are emphasized.

Keywords: organizational behavior, negative employee behavior, organizational deviance behavior, organizational silence, organizational cynicism, organizational justice

1. Introduction

When the organization and management literature is examined, it will be seen that it is full of concepts such as organizational citizenship behavior, positive organizational climate, organizational commitment, job satisfaction, and organizational identification. All these positive concepts are based on the assumption that human nature is compatible with external behavioral regulations and can be easily shaped. As Douglas McGregor mentioned in the X and Y theory, although some researchers claim the opposite, this positive view has continued. Organizational behavior researchers have had the goal of creating happy employees in the workplace, starting from the idea that "happy cows produce more milk." For this reason, organizational behavior research has focused on the positive aspects of organizational life [1–4]. At the same time, although some scholars have emphasized the dark side of organizational life, many researchers have focused on producing pragmatic tools for today's managers. The positive aspects of organizational life still dominate in organizational behavior (OB) research [5, 6]. However, it is not possible to isolate employees who are part of organizational life from negative emotions such as jealousy, anger, enmity, hatred, and revenge. From this point of view, some academics draw attention to the fact that the dynamics that shape the dark side actors of organizations can further explain the perspectives and behavioral structures of employees. Another point that should not be overlooked is that this dark side that emerges in organizations is a double-sided coin consisting of employees and managers [7, 8]. It is sometimes the practices of the managers that bring the dark side of organizational behavior to light, and sometimes it can be caused by the personality traits of the employees. Sometimes, the inappropriate use of power by managers causes negative behaviors in organizations, while negatively affecting the interaction between managers and employees.

Weber confirmed the existence of Weberian pessimism about the negative consequences of the domination of organizations filled with legal rational authority on societies and Coleman [6] following this historical transformation. This transformation changes social relations and individuals interact not only with individuals but also with organizations and other organizations in their organizations as before. Coleman's first prediction on this subject is that the structural transformation in question leads to both perceived and real loss of power for individuals. But the rise of these formal organizations has also opened up new possibilities for negative societal consequences, as error, abuse, and destruction have brought forth [9]. Surprisingly, however, the harmful actions caused by the dark side of organizations and the far-reaching social costs to the public have not been recognized as central to the field of sociologists, whose expertise is defined as organizations, professions, and work. Organizational sociologists have argued that formal organizations may deviate from the rationalist expectations of the Weberian model and that mainstream organizational theories are part of pathologies that harm organizational members [10, 11]. At the same time, organizational sociologists have been working on defining the dark side of organizations for a long time and have a lot of knowledge about how things go wrong in organizations. But without theories of organizational behavior, all of the socially organized conditions that produced harmful consequences remained obscure. All these reasons reveal the need to clarify the dark side of organizations with interdisciplinary studies.

The main source of interest in the dark side of organizational behavior is the negative consequences and destructive effects of the negative effects of the negative attitudes and behaviors of the human resources, which are vital for organizations, in the organization. Evaluating this emerging picture, it is thought that the dark side of organizations, which is a new and often overlooked phenomenon, should be included in the center of current organizational theory. This phenomenon will contribute to organizational theory in its new and analytical solutions to cope with the negativities it will create in organizations. At this point, considering the permeability between borders, it is important to evaluate an alternative critical perspective to the mainstream organizational theory together, in terms of determining the place of the dark sides of organizations in organizational behavior. Information about the dark side of organizations, within and between disciplines, can be considered in four categories.

- First, the contrasts and similarities in the studies on the subject are not clear. However, the theoretical framework for discussion has not been determined and there is no dialog necessary for intellectual development.
- Second, the importance of both the social origins and organizational consequences of harmful organizational behaviors has not been fully elucidated.
- Third, the sociological basis of policy implications for organizations, the public, and agents of social control is not yet developed.
- Finally, there is a broader theoretical background [9].

These different approaches are important arguments that can be used to understand, evaluate, and compare the dark side of organizations. Organizational theories and organizational behavior theories, which are shaped within the framework of rational human behaviors, have been deeply shaken by the dark side of organizational behavior, which is a reflection of irrational human behaviors [9]. This shift, which emerged at the baseline, needs to be handled carefully within the framework of its negative effects at the organizational level.

This study begins by examining the dark side of organizations and negative emotions among employees in the workplace. Emotions can have both positive and negative consequences in business. In the first systematic studies of the management literature, an emotion-free environment was constructed. With the devastating effects of the Great Depression, which emerged in the continuation of globalization and industrialization, the ignoring of emotions in the workplaces paid the price. After this initial shock was over, the intellectual movement sought to examine and explain emotions. Emotions have been classified by scientists in various ways, positive and negative. Thus, possible causes and consequences of positive and negative emotions were tried to be defined. Studies have proven that the psychological burden of negative emotions and events is at a higher level than expected. From this point of view, the organization in the background of the dark side of organizational behavior will be evaluated within the framework of theories, relations with variables, and solution proposals.

2. The dark side of organizational behavior

Throughout history, darkness and light have been used as metaphors to describe the conditions people live in, their state of consciousness, their deepest instinctual impulses, and the border between life and death. It is very ironic that this metaphor is being used today as a "dark side" metaphor to describe problems that are overlooked, suppressed, or ignored in the field of organization, along with traditional management studies. Organizations define the external economic environment as the source of emerging problems. What is overlooked here is the consequences of human behavior in organizations. From this point of view, it has enabled the redefinition of negative elements in mainstream organizational theory and behavior as external or externally driven. In the last two decades, it has been understood that the dark side has ceased to be an external phenomenon that affects organizational action, but rather defines the dark side within the boundaries of the organization [7].

Studies on the dark side of organizational behavior have evaluated the concept in the axis of systematic violence and aggression in the workplace. The scope of these alarming behaviors, which can be considered as abnormal and deviant, has expanded rapidly and gathered under the umbrella of dark side. This trend-oriented study by Griffin and O'Leary-Kelly [7] has been a turning point for behaviors that are expressed as the dark side of organizational behavior. This study focuses on functional or dysfunctional ambiguous and motivated behaviors that contribute to people and organizational processes [12]. Violence in the workplace, which is the mainstay of this perspective, includes concepts such as stress, aggression, sexual harassment, sexual discrimination, local violence that also affects the workplace, careerism, breach of psychological contract, incivility, and theft. It consists of situations where injustices are perpetuated, and the pursuit of wealth, power, or revenge leads people to unethical, illegal, despicable, or reprehensible behavior [7].

Many of the behaviors belonging to the dark side are difficult to understand and observe. For this reason, psychology, sociology, organizational behavior and so on have been investigated at different levels by different disciplines. The dark side of organizational behavior has become an inseparable part of the field by being theorized and in an increasing variety at the individual, group, and organizational level in recent years. Studies show that a wide variety of personal relationships in the workplace are compatible with the dark side framework from a negative point of view, but they are not named as such. At this point, it is seen that negative perspectives are closely related to dark side frameworks and there are studies that deal with different interpersonal relationships in the workplace [13]. While the individual oriented structures of the studies focus on dark side of leadership [14], deviant and counterproductive behaviors in the workplace [15–18], workplace violence and aggression [19, 20], interpersonal [21, 22], maltreatment workplace incivility [23] are the subjects.

In studies of the dark side, Ackroyd and Thompson [24] tried to go beyond accepting these behaviors as misbehaviors, deviations, or oppositional resistance while reclassifying the relationships between deviant behaviors that occur in various ways from the traditional perspective. Vaughan [1], who tries to look at the dark side of organizational behavior from a different perspective, states that the dark side can be accepted as "non-compliance with routine" and this acceptance will bring along three basic negative consequences called error, abuse, and destruction. However, it is stated that such behaviors are a result of routine systems and that it is a predictable and repetitive process not only in organizations but also in all social systems. However, dark side behaviors are influenced by environmental and organizational factors. Environmental factors include innovation, competition, growth factors, and imitability, while organizational factors generally include structure, processes, and tasks. In addition, socio-cognitive factors should be considered in the evaluations of the dark side [9].

One of the studies with a different perspective is the study by Ackroyd and Thompson [24] in which they openly criticize mainstream organizational behavior approaches. Here is an individualistic understanding of rationality and the illusion of organizational behavior that "if something can be understood, it can be managed." Vardi and Wiener's emphasis on primarily concrete covers not only psychological analysis but also sociological approaches. The point here is that organizational politics stems from the conflict of "unequal power and structural resources," collectively shared and opposing interests. This point of view is considered to be somewhat sharp, even extremist, for organizational behavior. Management processes and workplace rationalities are not just top-down. Resistance to undesirable practices hides the bad behaviors that occur in the organization in a very different way. However, their purpose in bringing this to light is to complicate understanding rather than merely improving performance.

When the dark side is evaluated not only at the organizational but also at the individual level, the acceptance that the darkness may be deeply rooted in the inner world of the individual can bring a different perspective to the subject. It is a reality that we do not want to accept the fact that repressed or hidden disturbing desires, motivations can lead individuals to lie, cheat, steal, bully, and even kill someone. This inner dark side that we try to deny is associated with organizational violence [22, 25]. The existence and impact of this institutional psychopathology has been explored especially since the 2002–2003 ethical crisis and the 2007–2008 financial crisis [26–29]. Griffin and O'Leary-Kelly [7] want to illuminate the current dilemmas of organizations with their work without creating a simple contrast between dark and light. This desire is to provide a positive contribution to the improvement of organizational functioning and the experience of people working within organizations.

Later on, it was concluded that "the organizational aspects typically associated with the bright side are also on the dark side." In this outcome, environmental factors include innovation, imitability, growth factors, and the ability or strength to compete for scarce resources, while organizational factors broadly encompass structure, processes, and tasks; it also considers socio-cognitive factors. The dark side is included in the light side as "structural bonds" at the environmental level. Three circles are mentioned together with the patterns and their origins [9]. These environments emerge in characteristic forms at the organizational and socio-cognitive level. Accordingly, it is thought that the sharing of concepts among the fields of interest and at the same time the reevaluation of the empirical emphasis between the fields will enrich the theoretical structure of the dark side. On this plane, dark-side behavior may be negative, abnormal, or even deviant from an organizational point of view, but they do not tend to stereotype or stigmatize behaviors, groups, and actors, recognizing that these behaviors may appear normal, rational when observed from different perspectives and with different tools [7]. It will enable organizational action to be taken to eliminate the causes of undesirable behavior belonging to the dark side and improve its consequences.

According to the results obtained from the studies conducted on the dark side, they organize their dark side behaviors into two broad categories, those that harm others and those that harm the organization, and each of these is further divided into two subcategories.

2.1 Behaviors toward harming others and self

Behaviors in this category are primarily and directly aimed at harming oneself or others. We can express these as two subheadings [7].

a. Toward Others

- Psychological Violence (Verbal/Verbal)

- Physical Violence

- Sexual Harassment
- General Unsafe Work Behaviors

a. Self-Oriented:

- Alcohol and Illegal Drug Use
- Smoking
- Private Unsafe Business Behaviors
- Suicide Attempt

2.2 The dark side of harmful behavior to the organization

In this category, negative behaviors aimed primarily at harming the organization itself are included, and harming human welfare is secondary. These are as follows:

a. Behaviors Causing Certain Financial Costs:

- Inappropriate absenteeism and being late for work
- Theft against organizational property or property
- Damage to organization property or property
- Violating laws, rules, and regulations
- Disruptive behaviors

b. Behaviors that do not cause definite financial costs:

- Political behavior
- Inappropriate impression management behaviors
- Violation of privacy
- Persistent poor performance

The dark side of organizational behavior is very comprehensive, and it has been seen in the literature that negative work behaviors are defined by various intertwined concepts. Gruys ([30]:40) stated in his literature review that he achieved over 250 anti-goal work behaviors. This result is important in terms of showing that the concept takes place in a very wide range. In this context, behaviors that are defined as the dark side of organizational behavior in the organizational behavior literature and that have negative consequences can be grouped under some headings. Definitions of some of these are given below.

Anti-Production Behaviors: These are conscious behaviors that have harmful effects on the organization and its members. These behaviors consist of active and passive actions and acts aimed at committing crimes. It includes active actions such as theft or aggression, and passive actions such as deliberately disobeying instructions or doing wrong work [31].

Mobbing: It can be defined as systematic, non-metric hostile communication by one or more people in the workplace against another employee [32].

Workplace Rudeness: Workplace incivility is defined as low-intensity deviant behavior with a goal-directed, ambiguous intention that goes against the norms of mutual respect in the work environment. Unpolite behavior is considered rude behavior that includes disrespect for others [33].

Cynical Behaviors: It is the negative attitude of the employee toward the organization. The belief that the organization lacks integrity is characterized by negative affect toward the organization, and a tendency to be condescending and critical toward the organization consistent with this belief and affect [34].

Sexual Harassment: Any undesirable verbal, non-verbal or physical conduct of a sexual nature that violates or influences the dignity of a person, especially by creating an intimidating, hostile, humiliating, embarrassing, and offensive environment [35].

Organizational Silence: Employee silence is the deliberate concealment of meaningful information, suggestions, questions, and concerns that can be used for the benefit of the organization [36]. Employee silence has direct (deprivation of information provided by the employee in solving operational problems, decrease in innovation, etc.) and indirect (such as stress and health problems in the employee) costs to the organization [37].

Careerism: Employees use methods such as establishing good relationships, advertising, and deceptive behaviors to pretend to be successful, instead of performance-based methods for career advancement. These employees have a tendency to harm the organization or its members when necessary [38].

Social Loafing Behavior: Social loafing is defined as the tendency of individuals to exert less effort when working in groups than when working individually [39].

Cyberloafing: It is defined as the employee's use of the internet connection of the institution he/she works for personal purposes during business hours and is considered as a behavior of deviation from production [40].

Revenge Behaviors: It is expressed as punishment in return for the wrong behavior perceived by the employee. Revenge behavior is shown among the main causes of aggressive behavior [41].

Gossip and Rumor: It is an informal form of communication conveyed to another person or persons, regardless of whether it actually exists or not. Rumor or gossip can have positive or negative consequences [42].

Destructive Political Behaviors: Political behavior is the use of force to influence others in the organization, to secure personal or collective interests, or to avoid negative situations in the organization. While political behaviors have positive benefits for the organization in some cases, they also have negative consequences. For example, when a manager promotes a friend with lower qualifications than other candidates, this dysfunctional behavior will cost the organization [7].

3. Approaches to explain the dark side of organizational behavior

According to Griffin and O'Leary-Kelly [7], the dark side of organizational behavior is defined as the behaviors performed by an employee or group in the organization with the motivation to have negative consequences for them. The authors divide the motivation for the emergence of the dark side of behavior into two. The first is the desire for negative consequences of behavior to occur. These results are measurable (such as direct theft and making a non-optimal organizational decision due to an indirect personal situation/agenda). The second is that the individual or individuals have the intention or awareness to show the behavior because of the consequences of this behavior. In this context, it is necessary to separate simple human errors from such behavior. Vaughan [9] in his article on the dark side of organizations stated that examining the dark sides of organizations is to reveal the functional inadequacy of the institutional foundations of the society. He stated that his routine non-compliance, mistake, misconduct, and inadequate behavior are not abnormal, but the product of complex structures and processes. He emphasized that the dark side of behavior is systematically produced by the interconnection between environment, organizations, cognition, and choice, which includes both unintentional and willing outcomes. The author stated that behavior is rational in situational contexts and that the social context can break the link between rational choice and its consequences. That's why organizations he claimed that it can produce unpredictable negative (negative) results that will cause deviation from determined goals, normative standards, and expectations.

The term dark side is actually a relative term. Even if it means a negative deviation from the targeted reference point, it is important what the deviation actually means here. For example, resistance to change can be "negative" even for those who advocate change. Because if change takes place, they may lose their jobs [10, 11, 43]. Therefore, the dark side of anything is relative and positional. To accommodate this relativity it was important that the study be as comprehensive as possible. To this end, the literature focuses on the connections between definitions and outcomes that can often be seen as counter to the core values, interests, or goals of the various stakeholders in the organization and its environment.

As it can be understood from the definition, the complicated structure of the dark side of organizational behavior and the ability to direct attitudes and behaviors require a wide range of evaluation of the field. Different theories and approaches are used to explain the complex structure created by these various fields.

In the reductionist approach, positivist organizational approaches, which rationally model organizations, and therefore organizational members, in the context of cause-effect relationship, left the studies on the dark side of the human factor that can act irrationally incomplete [9]. The stated shortcoming is related to the fact that studies in the field of organizational behavior generally center positive employee behaviors. However, it is important to understand the dark side of organizational behavior in order to integrate and direct employees from different personality traits and different cultures with organizational goals.

Theories and approaches explaining the dark side of organizational behavior vary due to the complex nature of the concept. In the literature review, it is seen that social commitment, expectation, empowerment, social learning, social information processing, frustration-aggression, emotional events and agency theories, and causal reasoning and stress-loading emotion model are used to explain the dark structure of organizational behavior.

a. *Social Learning Theory:* The theory developed by Bandura, individuals who receive positive/positive feedback for aggressive actions learn to exhibit aggressive behaviors. The theory attributes the causes of aggression to external factors rather than internal factors (instinct) and states that aggression is learned through direct experience and imitation, as in other behaviors [44].

b. *Frustration-Aggression Theory*: It accepts the theory's definition of aggression as a reactive behavior, not instinctive. The basic premise of the theory is the assumption that when goal-directed behavior is inhibited, it will lead to aggression. The inhibition in question may come from the person's environment, or it may occur as a result of contradictory wishes and tendencies within himself. Tendency to aggression is determined by the frequency and intensity of disruptive experiences [45]. Fox and Spector [46] found a positive relationship between anti-productive behaviors in organizations and organizational restraint (prevention of achieving personal and organizational goals).

c. *Causal Reasoning Theory:* The theory was developed by Martinko, Gundlach and Douglas [47]. They argue that counterproductive behaviors have two perspectives in common. These are beliefs about how individuals evaluate the quality of their outcomes (justice, equality, success, or failure) and attribution and attribution behaviors toward the causes of their outcomes. This is a two-stage cognitive process. Individuals evaluate their outputs in terms of their qualities, by making a kind of comparison. As a result of the evaluation, they perceive the situation as unbalanced, unjust, or unequal. This perception includes analyzing the causes of the situation and referring as a result. The main focus of the model is on what causes the outputs to be attributed, in terms of the nature and nature of anti-production behavior. If the person is referring to their own internal characteristics (such as lack of effort) when faced with a disappointing result, the individual will be more likely to blame himself. As a result of this reference, it will not engage in anti-production work behavior. However, depending on the individual's internal attribution, negative feelings about himself (shame and guilt) may reveal behaviors such as depression, alcohol, drug use, absenteeism, and poor performance. If the individual makes external references to causing frustration, they will be much more likely to demonstrate some of their anti-productive behavior (aggression, violence, harassment, sabotage, theft, vandalism, fraud).

d. *The Stressor-Emotion Model:* The model is based on the frustration-aggression theory. It predicts that anti-productive behavior is a response to situations that provoke frustration and anger. In the model, counterproductive behaviors begin with a situation that causes stress at work (role ambiguity, role conflict, workload, interpersonal conflict, organizational constraints, unfair practices, etc.). The individual perceives this situation as a stress factor and feels negative emotions (disability, anxiety, anger, etc.). These negative emotions are reflected as anti-production behavior. Stress factor is defined as an environmental situation that causes a negative emotional response in the individual. In addition, the model took perceived control and personality traits (trait anger and anxiety, narcissism, locus of control) as moderator/mediator variables. It has been stated that these mediator/regulatory variables have important contributions in demonstrating the anti-production behavior [47].

As can be seen, the complex structure of the dark side of organizational behavior has been tried to be explained within the framework of different theories. However, historical, sociological, psychological, and organizational studies have been systematically categorized in order to legitimize the theoretical framework regarding the dark side of organizations [7]. Similarly, a number of contemporary psychological studies on the dark side of organizational behavior have been brought together. In light of these studies, international trade [48] and social capital [49, 50] are among the external issues related to the dark side of organizational behavior. Other studies have been conducted on the dark side of management excellence [51], leadership [52], entrepreneurship [53–56], management decisions [50, 57, 58]. Some of these studies focused on executive psychology [59–61] and leadership [14, 62, 63]. However, Linstead, Maréchal, Griffin [64], and Bella, King, Kailin [65] have made methodological contributions to revealing the dark side.

4. Antecedents of the dark side of organizational behavior

Many factors are effective in the negative attitudes and behaviors of employees in organizations. In this context, it is possible to categorize the antecedents of dark behavior in terms of personal characteristics and situational factors (organizational, social, and interpersonal factors). When the literature is examined, it has been revealed that employees with anger and anxiety orientation, revenge-oriented attitude, negative affect, low self-control, tendency to bad intentions, negative past experience, narcissistic, psychopathic, Machiavellian personality traits have a higher tendency to exhibit negative organizational behavior [66–68]. The sub-dimensions of the concept, which is defined as the dark triad in the organizational behavior literature, are grouped as Machiavellian, narcissistic, and psychopathic personality traits. In the meta-analysis study conducted to reveal the relationships between these personality traits and job performance and anti-production behavior. It has been found that employees with these three personality traits have high anti-production behavior and low job performance [68]. Similarly, Bushman [69] revealed that high self-esteem and high narcissism produce the highest level of aggression. In another study evaluating the relationship between organizational deviant behaviors and demographic variables, it was determined that generally male, single, young, newly employed, part-time workers, lower education level, and those working in low paid positions were more prone to organizational deviance behaviors [67, 70]. It is thought that individuals who exhibit dark behavior in organizations have some common characteristics. However, studies have shown that this is not true and the strong roles of contextual factors. It can be said that some personality traits make individuals more reactive, and individuals with this trait are more success-oriented in a certain organizational environment [71, 72].

The organizational factors that are generally effective in the emergence of negative organizational behaviors include perceived injustice, inequality, role ambiguity, role conflict, high workload, low autonomy, low job autonomy, lack of job security, interpersonal conflict, organizational constraints, organizational structure, organizational culture and climate, organizational policy and processes, leadership style, working conditions, wage, promotion, and career opportunities [71, 73, 74].

Therefore, the situations that cause the perception of stress and frustration in the organization, together with other variables, may be a factor in the negative behavior of the employees toward the organization. In this context, they are listed below for a more concrete understanding of the subject.

The perception of injustice, which is one of the antecedents of the dark side of organizations, is important in terms of organizational results. Employees who perceive that they are exposed to injustice and unequal treatment by their organizations will want to eliminate this injustice. These reactions of employees generally reflect to third parties outside the employer-employee relationship (colleagues, customers, shareholders, general public), and over time, employees begin to behave reactively [75]. For this reason, while the focus of organizational justice research is organizational outcomes, contemporary studies seem to focus on employee responses, the dark side of injustice [76]. When employees are faced with injustice, their commitment decreases, their absenteeism increases, and their desire to quit their job arises. This situation can reach dimensions that can harm the organization with the decrease in performance. The perception of injustice also triggers the aggression behaviors of the employees with the feeling of revenge, and in a way, it is the response given to the organization against injustice through behaviors such as sabotage, opposing the business rules, and theft [77]. Apart from this, employees may show a tendency to rebuild justice by themselves in order to eliminate the perception of injustice. Accordingly, the tendency to show negative behaviors such as revenge, theft, and idleness increases [78, 79]. At the same time, injustice triggers organizational cynicism. While there is a negative relationship between organizational justice and cynical attitudes [79–81], he states that employees' perceptions of injustice increase cynical feelings. It is one of the results of the study by Bateman, Sakono, and Fujita [82] that employees with a perception of unfairness are bored, skeptical, and insecure. Similarly, James [81] and Anderson [83] reveal in their study that organizational cynicism attitudes increase as the organizational justice perception of employees decreases. Organizational cynicism is a common way of expressing dissatisfaction toward their organization [84–86] and they stated that cynics harbor skepticism toward the organization and display frustration, dissatisfaction, and hatred toward the organization. In addition, academics stated that organizational cynicism is a situation variable and that organizational practices and policies can affect the attitudes of employees. According to cognitive behavioral theory and social exchange theory, employees' negative perceptions of the organization will produce corresponding coping behaviors. Based on the principle of reciprocity, a hostile exchange of resources is not conducive to the relationship between members of the organization. For example, these attitudes may affect turnover intention and organizational commitment. As a result, organizational cynicism is detrimental to organizational performance and achievement of goals [87]. However, injustice is a factor that can be effective in the silence of employees. If the employees have the perception that the decision-making mechanisms and practices in the organization are fair, this perception is a motivating factor for the employees to eliminate the silence [88]. Studies conducted in this context are of a nature that reveals the existence of a relationship between silence and organizational justice [89–91]. In addition, Pinder [92] found in his study that employees became silent as a reaction against organizational injustice, and silence emerged as a resistance against injustice. However, the results of the research on silence reveal that the perception of high justice distracts the employees from the silence behavior [93]. Fair behavior of the management within the framework of ethical and moral principles will reduce the level of personal fears of the employees and will encourage them to talk about the problems in the organization.

However, there is a positive relationship between workplace incivility, which is the violation of the norm of mutual respect, avoidance orientation, and organizational climate [75]. When evaluating the subject within the framework of social and interpersonal factors, various elements such as stress and anxiety, resulting from factors like a lack of control, uncertain work conditions, economic conditions, family problems, alcohol and drug use, and social status, contribute to the emergence of dark behaviors [70, 73, 94, 95].

5. Consequences of the dark side of behavior in organizations

The dark side of behavior leads to violent behavior in the workplace. This violence can be psychological as well as physical violence in some cases. These can range from simple arguments to killing a colleague. The fact that violence caused by dark side behavior accounts for 10% of workplace deaths in the United States (2004) reveals the gravity of the situation. It is stated that the number of American workers exposed to physical movement such as hitting, pushing ect. is more than 2 million per year [96].

Negative consequences of dark behavior can be analyzed at three different levels: individual, organizational, and societal. In addition, as mentioned before, every behavior that affects the employee also affects the organization. Negative effects of dark behaviors on the employee; loss of motivation, decrease in performance, decrease in creativity, decrease in self-esteem, depression, irritability, anxiety, negative thoughts, burnout, excessive anger and stress [72]. This situation can cause physical and psychological diseases, smoking, alcohol and drug abuse, occupational accidents, disability, and suicides in employees [97]. Studies have found that there are serious deteriorations in the health of employees who are exposed to violence in the workplace caused by the dark side of organizational behavior. In addition, sleep disorders, musculoskeletal complaints, and post-traumatic stress disorder are observed [72].

Studies reveal that there are serious deteriorations1 in the health of employees who are exposed to workplace violence caused by the dark side of organizational, behavior. However, sleep disorders, musculoskeletal complaints, and post-traumatic stress disorder are seen [72]. It has been determined that the level of stress seen in those exposed to violence in the workplace is higher than the level of post-traumatic stress seen in recently divorced, war zone personnel, etc. [34, 98]. One of the important consequences of violence in business life is employee burnout. Burnout, which can be expressed as "the depletion of mental and physical energy in the individual," affects not only his work life but also his whole life negatively by depersonalizing the individual physically and spiritually [99].

The dark side of organizational behavior causes negative results in employee relations, work order and work environment in the near and far periods of organizations. From an organizational point of view, it has direct and indirect effects. The direct costs include absenteeism and turnover, accidents, diseases, disabilities, death, and the development of safety systems. On the other hand, indirect costs are equally important and can lead to decrease in productivity, deterioration in product quality, loss of image in the institution, decrease in the number of customers, decrease in the actions that are beneficial to the organization such as organizational commitment, creativity, and organizational citizenship behaviors of the employees. Therefore, the effectiveness and efficiency of the organization is negatively affected [100, 101]. The negative effects of dark behavior on society include economic losses and sociocultural effects such as increase in health expenses, loss of workforce, and disability. It has been revealed that negative behaviors in the workplace not only affect the physical and psychological health of employees, but also negatively affect family life and quality of life by creating work-family conflict. In this context, it can be said that the relational context of bad behavior in the workplace exceeds the boundaries of the organization and negatively affects the whole society [72].

Clarifying this dilemma that organizations are in will increase the organizational functionality and positive contributions of employees to the organization. At the same time, identifying and eliminating the causes of dark side behaviors is important in terms of carrying out organizational actions and improving results. Organizations today operate in an unpredictable and complex environment. This unpredictability and complexity constantly affects the employment relationship between the organization and employees, along with organizational changes. This situation negatively affects the attitudes and behaviors of employees, which is one of the important factors in achieving organizational success. Negative attitudes and behaviors of employees who are active in organizational success not only decrease organizational performance, but also cause reform resistance and harm the development of the organization.

Author details

Semra Köse
Department of Business Administration, Istanbul Aydin University, Turkey

*Address all correspondence to: kose.semra@gmail.com

References

[1] Vaughan D. Analytic ethnography. In: Hedstrom P, Barman P, editors. The Oxford Handbook of Analytical Sociology. Oxford: Oxford University Press; 2009. pp. 688-711

[2] Scott WR. Organizations. 4th ed. Upper Saddle River, NJ: Prentice Hall; 1998

[3] Anheier H, editor. When Things Go Wrong. Thousand Oaks, CA: Sage; 1998

[4] Bamberger PA, Sonnenstuhl WJ. Research in the Sociology of Organizations: Deviance in and of Organizations. Vol. 15. Stamford, CT: JAI Press Inc; 1998

[5] Speedy S. Workplace violence: The dark side of organisational life. Contemporary Nurse. 2006;**21**(2):239-250

[6] Coleman JS. Power and the Structure of Society. Philadelphia: Univ. Phila. Press; 1974

[7] Griffin RW, O'Leary-Kelly AM. The Dark Side of Organizational Behaviour. San Francisco: Jossey-Bass; 2004

[8] Manning P. The dark side of social capital: Lessons from the Madoff case. In: Sun W, Stewart J, Pollard D, editors. Reframing Corporate Social Responsibility: Lessons from the Global Financial Crisis (Critical Studies on Corporate Responsibility, Governance and Sustainability, Volume 1). Bingley: Emerald Group Publishing Limited; 2010. pp. 207-228

[9] Vaughan D. The dark side of organizations: Mistake, misconduct, and disaster. Annual Review of Sociology. 1999;**25**:271-305

[10] Hall R. Organizations. 6th ed. Englewood Cliffs, NJ: Prentice Hall; 1996

[11] Perrow C. Complex Organizations. 3rd. ed. New York: Random House; 1986

[12] Griffin RW, Lopez YP. 'Bad behavior' in organizations: A review and typology for future research. Journal of Management. 2005;**31**:988-1005

[13] de Eby LTT, Allen TD. Personal Relationships: The Effect on Employee Attitudes, Behaviour and Well-Being. New York: Taylor & Francis; 2012

[14] Tourish D. The Dark Side of Transformational Leadership: A Critical Perspective. London: Routledge; 2013

[15] Hodson R, Jensen GF. Conceptual Foundations. In: Deviant and criminal behavior in the workplace. New York University Press; 2013. pp. 3-16

[16] Bordia P, Restubog SLD, Tang RL. When employees strike back: Investigating mediating mechanisms between psychological contract breach and workplace deviance. Journal of Applied Psychology. 2008;**93**:1104-1117

[17] Branch S, Ramsay S, Barker M. Workplace bullying, mobbing and general harassment: A review. International Journal of Management Reviews. 2013;**15**:280-299

[18] Treadway DC, Shaughnessy BA, Breland JW, Yang J, Reeves M. Political skill and the job performance of bullies. Journal of Managerial Psychology. 2013;**28**(3):273-289. DOI: 10.1108/02683941311321169

[19] Hitlan RT. Workplace Violence and Aggression: The

Dark Side of Organizations. In: Kelloway EK, Barling J, Hurrell JJ, Jr., editors. Handbook of workplace violence. PsycCRITIQUES. 2006;**51**(45). DOI: 10.1037/a0004307

[20] Glomb TM, Liao H. Interpersonal aggression in work groups: Social influence, reciprocal, and individual effects. Academy of Management Journal. 2003;**46**:486-496

[21] Ragins BR, Cornwell JM. Pink triangles: Antecedents and consequences of perceived workplace discrimination against gay and lesbian employees. Journal of Applied Psychology. 2001;**86**:1244-1261

[22] Kristeva, J. (1982). Powers of Horror: An Essay on Abjection. Translated by L. S. Roudiez. New York: Columbia University Press

[23] Bjørkelo B. Workplace bullying after whistleblowing: Future research and implications. Journal of Managerial Psychology. 2013;**28**:306-323

[24] Ackroyd S, Thompson P. Organizational Misbehaviour. London: Routledge; 1999

[25] Linstead SA. Death in Vegas: Seduction, kitsch, and sacrifice. M@n@gement. 2001;**4**:159-174

[26] Babiak P, Hare RD. Snakes in Suits: When Psychopaths Go to Work. New York: Harper Collins; 2006

[27] Boddy CR. Corporate psychopaths and organisational type. Journal of Public Affairs. 2010;**10**:300-312

[28] Boddy CR, Galvin PG, Ladyshewsky R. Leaders without ethics in global business: Corporate psychopaths. Journal of Public Affairs. 2010;**10**:121-138

[29] Linstead SA. Organizational kitsch. Organization. 2002;**9**:657-684

[30] Gruys, M L. The Dimensionality of Deviant Employee Performance in the Workplace. Unpublished Doctoral Dissertation, Phd Thesis, Human Resources and Industrial Relations in the Graduate School University of Minnesota, 1999:144

[31] Fox S, Spector P, ve Miles, D. Counterproductive work behavior in response to job stressors and organizational justice: Some mediator and moderator tests for autonomy and emotions. Journal of Vocational Behavior. 2001;**59**:291-309

[32] Leymann H. Mobbing and psychological terror at workplaces. Violence and Victims. 1990;**5**(2):119-126

[33] Andersson LM, Pearson CM. Tit for tat? The spiraling effect of incivility in the workplace. Academy of Management Review. 1999;**24**(3):452-471

[34] Dean JW, Brandes P, Dhwardkar R. Organizational cynicism. Academy of Management Review. 1998;**23**(2):341-352

[35] European Commission (EC). Harassment related to Sex and Sexual Harassment Law in 33 European Countries (Ann Numhauser-Henning and Sylvaine Laulom). 2012. Available from: http://ec.europa.eu/justice/genderequality/files/your_rights/final_harassement_en.pdf

[36] Tangirala S, Ramanujam R. Employee silence on critical work issues: The cross level effects of procedural justice climate. Personnel Psychology. 2008;**61**:37-68

[37] Knoll M, Van Dick R. Do I hear the whistle...? A first attempt to measure four forms of employee silence and their

correlates. Journal of Busşness Ethics. 2013;**113**:349-362

[38] Feldman DC, Weitz BA. From the invisible hand to the gladhand: Understanding a careerist orientation to work. Human Resource Management. 1991;**30**(2):237-257

[39] Karau SJ, Williams KD. Social loafing: A meta-analytic review and theoretical integration. Journal of Personality and Social Psychology. 1993;**65**(4):681-706

[40] Lim VKG. The IT way of loafing on the job: Cyberloafing. Neutralizing and organizational justice. Journal of Organizational Behavior. 2002;**23**:675-694

[41] Bradfield M, Aquino K. The effects of blame attributions and offender likableness on forgiveness and revenge in the workplace. Journal of Management. 1999;**25**(5):607-631

[42] Michelson G, Mouly S. Do loose lips sink ships?: The meaning, antecedents and consequences of rumour and gossip in organisations. Corporate Communications: An International Journal. 2004;**9**(3):189-201

[43] Coleman JW, Ramos LL. Subcultures and Deviant Behavior in the Organizational Context. Research in the Sociology of Organizations. 1998;**15**:3-34

[44] O'Leary-Kelly AM, Griffin RW, Glew DJ. Organization-motivated aggression: A research framework. Academy of Management Review. 1996;**21**(1):225-253

[45] Dollard J, Doob L, Miller N, Mowrer O, Sears R. Frustration and Aggression. New Haven, CT: Yale University Press; 1939. DOI: 10.1037/10022-000

[46] Fox S, Spector P. A model of work frustration-aggression. Journal of Organizational Behavior. 1999;**20**:915-931

[47] Martinko MJ, Gundlach MJ, Douglas SC. Toward an integrative theory of counterproductive workplace behavior: A casual reasoning perspective. International Journal of Selection and Assessment. 2002;**10**(1/2):36-50

[48] Batra MM. The dark side of international business. Competition Forum. 2007;**5**:306-314

[49] Graeff P. Social capital: The dark side. In: Svendsen GT, Svendsen GLH, editors. Handbook of Social Capital. Cheltenham, UK: Edward Elgar; 2009. pp. 143-161

[50] Virtanen P, Lehtonen T, Raisio H. Reaching into the dark side of organisations: The banality and emergence of administrative evil in the light of two case examples. Scandinavian Journal of Public Administration. 2022;**26**(2):3-21

[51] Dunning D. The dark side of excellence. The Effective Leader. 1998;**3**:1-4

[52] Dromantaite A. The dark side of leadership in the organization: What it is and how to control it. LOGOS-VILNIUS. 2022;**112**:201-208

[53] Haynes KT, Hitt MA, Campbell JT. The dark side of leadership: Towards a mid-range theory of hubris and greed in entrepreneurial contexts. Journal of Management Studies. 2015;**52**(4):479-505

[54] Khan FR, Munir KA, Willmott H. A dark side of institutional entrepreneurship: Soccer balls, child labour and postcolonial impoverishment. Organization Studies. 2007;**28**:1055-1077

[55] Beaver G, Jennings P. Competitive advantage and entrepreneurial power:

The dark side of entrepreneurship. Journal of Small Business and Enterprise Development. 2005;**12**:9-23

[56] Kets de & Vries, M. F. R. The dark side of entrepreneurship. Harvard Business Review. 1985;**85**:160-167

[57] Debre MJ. The dark side of regionalism: How regional organizations help authoritarian regimes to boost survival. Democratization. 2021;**28**(2):394-413

[58] Boddy CR. The dark side of management decisions: Organisational psychopaths. Management Descision. 2006;**44**:1461-1475

[59] Bollaert H, Petit V. Beyond the dark side of executive psychology: Current research and new directions. European Management Journal. 2010;**28**:362-376

[60] Judge T, LePine J. The bright and dark sides of personality. In: Langan-Fox J, Cooper C, Klimoski R, editors. Research Companion to the Dysfunctional Workplace. Cheltenham, UK: Edward Elgar; 2007. pp. 332-355

[61] Judge TA, Piccolo RF, Kosalka T. The bright and dark sides of leader traits: A review and theoretical extension of the leader trait paradigm. Leadership Quarterly. 2009;**20**:855-875

[62] Harms PD, Spain SM, Hannah ST. Leader development and the dark side of personality. Leadership Quarterly. 2011;**22**:495-509

[63] Clements C, Washbrush JB. The two faces of leadership: Considering the dark side of leaderfollower dynamics. Journal of Workplace Learning. 1999;**11**:170-176

[64] Linstead S, Maréchal G, Griffin RW. Theorizing and researching the dark side of organization. Organization Studies. 2014;**35**(2):165-188

[65] Bella DA, King JB, Kailin D. The dark side of organizations and a method to reveal it. Emergence. 2003;**5**:66-82

[66] Douglas SC, Martinko MJ. Exploring the role of individual differences in the prediction of workplace aggression. Journal of Applied Psychology. 2001;**86**:547-559

[67] Hauge LJ, Skogstad A, Einarsen S. Individual and situational predictors of workplace bullying: Why do perpetrators engage in the bullying of others? Work & Stress. 2009;**23**:349-358

[68] O'Boyle EH Jr, Forsyth DR, Banks GC, McDaniel MA. A meta-analysis of the dark triad and work behavior: A social exchange perspective. Journal of Applied Psychology. 2012, 2012;**97**(3):557-579

[69] Bushman BJ, Baumeister RF, Thomaes S, Ryu E, Begeer S, West SG. Looking again, and harder, for a link between low self-esteem and aggression. Journal of Personality. 2009;**77**:427-446

[70] Appelbaum SH, Deguire KJ, Lay M. The relationship of ethical climate to deviant workplace behavior. Corporate Governance. 2005;**5**(4):43-55

[71] Spector PE, Fox S. The Stressor-Emotion Model of Counterproductive Work Behavior. In: Fox S, Spector PE, editors. Counterproductive work behavior: Investigations of actors and targets. American Psychological Association; 2005. pp. 151-174. DOI: 10.1037/10893-007

[72] Hershcovis MS, Reich TC, ve Niven K. Workplace bullying: Causes, consequences, and intervention strategies. In: SIOP White Paper Series. International Affairs Committee of the Society for Industrial and Organizational Psychology; 2015. pp. 1-22

[73] De Cuyper N, Baillien E, De Witte H. Job insecurity, perceived employability and targets' and perpetrators' experiences of workplace bullying. Work & Stress. 2009;**23**:206-224

[74] Everton WJ, Jolton JA, Mastrangelo PM. Be nice and fair or else: Understanding reasons for employee's deviant behaviors. Journal of Management Development. 2007;**26**(2):117-131

[75] Starlicki DP, ve Kulik, C.T. Third-party reactions to employee (mis) treatment: A justice perspective. Researchin Organizational Behavior. 2004;**26**:183-229

[76] Ambrose ML, Seabright MA, ve Schminke, M. Sabotage in the workplace: The role of organizational İnjustice. Organizational Behavior and Human Desicion Processes. 2002;**89**:974-965

[77] Poussard JM, Erkmen T. Yönetim, İletişim. Arıkan Yayınları: Kültür; 2008

[78] Nayir KF. Öğretmen Adaylarının Öç Alma Davranışına İlişkin Görüşleri. Electronic Turkish Studies. 2015;**10**(11):1205-1216

[79] Bernerth JB, Armenakis AA, Feild HS, Walker H. Jack. Justice, cynicism, and commitment a study of important organizational change variables, The Journal of Applied Behavioral Science. September 2007;**43**(3):303-326

[80] Johnson JL, O'leary-Kelly AM. The effects of psychological contract breach and organizational cynicism: Not all social exchange violations are created equal. Journal of Organizational Behavior. 2003;**24**:627-647

[81] James Matrecia SL. Antecedents and consequences of cynicismin organizations: an examination of the potential positive and negative effects on school systems. [Unpublished Doctoral Dissertation] The Florida State University, USA. 2005

[82] Bateman TS, Sakano T, ve Fujita, M. Roger, me, and my attitude: Film propaganda and cynicism toward corporate leadership. Journal of Applied Psychology. 1992;**77**(5):768

[83] Haynes KT, Hitt MA, Campbell JT. The dark side of leadership: Towards a mid-range theory of hubris and greed in entrepreneurial. Journal of Management Studies. 2015;**52**(4):479-505

[84] Andersson LM. Employee cynicism: An examination using a contract violation framework. Human Relations. 1996;**49**(11):ss. 1395-ss. 1418

[85] Chan M. Organizational justice theories and landmark cases. International Journal of Organizational Analysis. 2000;**8**(1):68-88. DOI: 10.1108/eb028911

[86] Chaburah DS, Peng AC, Oh I-S, Banks GC, Lomeli LC. Antecedents and consequences of employee organizational cynicism: A meta-analysis. Journal of Vocational Behavior. 2013;**83**(2):181-197

[87] Nafei WA, Kaifi BA. The İmpact of organizational cynicism on organizational commitment: An applied study on teaching Hospitalsin Egypt. European Journal of Business and Management. 2013;**5**(12):132

[88] Pillai R, Schriesheimand CA, Williams ES. Fairness perceptions and trust as Mediatorsfor Transformationaland transactional leadership: A two sample study. Journal of Management. 1999;**25**(6):897-933

[89] Brinsfield CT. Employee Silence: Investigation of Dimensionality,

Development of Measures, and Examination of Related Factors Dissertation. Yayımlanmamış Doktora Tezi: Ohio State University; 2009

[90] Özdemir L, Uğur SS. Çalışanların Örgütsel Ses ve Sessizlik Algılamalarının Demografik Nitelikler Açısından Değerlendirilmesi: Kamu Ve Özel Sektörde Bir Araştırma. Atatürk Üniversitesi İktisadi ve İdari Bilimler Dergisi. 2013;**27**(1):257-281

[91] Dyne LV, Ang S, Botero IC. Conceptualizing employee silence and employee voice as multidimensional constructs. Journal of Management Studies. 2003;**40**(6):1359-1392

[92] Pinder CC, Harlos KP. Employee silence: Quiescence and acquiescence As responses to Perceivedinjustice. Research in Personnel and Human Resources Management. 2001;**20**:331-369

[93] Brinsfield CT. Employee silence motives: Investigation of dimensionality and development of measures. Journal of Organizational Behavior. 2013;**34**(5):671-697

[94] Pearson CM, Porath CL. The Cost of Bad Behavior: How Incivility Is Damaging your Business and What to Do about it. New York, NY: Penguin Group; 2009. Available from: https://books.google.com.tr/books?id=MUxAAb

[95] Appelbaum SH, Iaconi GD, Matousek A. Positive and negative deviant workplace behaviors: Causes, impacts, and solutions. Corporate Governance: The International Journal of Business in Society. 2007;**7**(5):586-598

[96] Fleet DDV, Griffin RW. Dysfunctional organization culture: The role of leadership in motivating dysfunctional work behaviors. Journal of Managerial Psychology. 2006;**21**(8):698-708

[97] Yıldız AN, Kaya M, Bilir M. İşyerinde Şiddet. Türkiye İşçi Sendikaları Konfederasyonu, Ziraat Grup Matbaacılık, Ankara: Hacettepe Üniversitesi Tıp Fakültesi Halk Sağlığı Anabilim Dalı; 2011. p. 54

[98] Matthiesen SB, ve Einarsen, S. Psychiatric distress and symptoms of PTSD among victims of bullying at work. British Journal of Guidance & Counselling. 2004;**32**(3):335-356

[99] Winnubst J. Organizational structure, social support, and burnout. In: Professional Burnout. CRC Press; 2017. pp. 151-162

[100] Kanten P. İşyeri Nezaketsizliğinin Sosyal Kaytarma Davranışı ve İşten Ayrılma Niyeti Üzerindeki Etkisinde Duygusal Tükenmenin Aracılık Rolü. Aksaray Üniversitesi İktisadi ve İdari Bilimler Fakültesi Dergisi. 2014;**6**(1):11-26

[101] Ariani DW. The relationship between employee engagement, organizational citizenship behavior, and counterproductive work behavior. International Journal of Business Administration. 2013;**4**(2):46-56

Chapter 3

Perspective Chapter: The Dark Triad in the Organization – A Review of the Evidence and Future Recommendations

Olga Lainidi, Vilma Chalili, Ilias Maliousis, Maria Spiliou, Eva Tzioti, Panagiota Koutsimani and Anthony Montgomery

Abstract

Individuals who score high on dark personality assessments are found in managerial positions and are more likely to get promoted. Congruently, abusive and toxic leadership is still tolerated in most industries; and many aspects of toxic organizational culture are maintained over time and interventions (e.g., bullying, employee silence). There is a gap in our understanding of how positive and negative elements of individuals interact in the workplaces. We review the existing evidence on how dark personality traits might be linked with positive and negative aspects of work-life and whether this evidence can help us answer the question how do dark personality traits help individuals get ahead at work? Finally, we propose implications for practice and directions for future research.

Keywords: dark personality traits, abusive supervision, organizational well-being, toxic leadership, empathy

1. Introduction

Over the past 25 years, organizational psychology has witnessed a renewed focus on concepts and ideas associated with positive psychology, as well as on what can make work environments better and work more efficient [1]. Identifying ways to make things better is certainly important and has contributed to the improvement of both the field and the quality of work environments in most professions and industries. However, the rush to incorporate more positive elements in research (e.g., job engagement, positive psychological capital) should not result in less attention to the robust negative work experiences that influence a range of organizational outcomes. In terms of organizational behavior, for example, the interest in employee voice behaviors—the genuine expression of concerns, ideas and thoughts to persons capable of effecting change [2]—preceded that of employee silence [2]. A brief search of the key terms "employee silence" and "employee voice" on some of the main research databases is indicative of the differences in how long the productive (voice) and unproductive (silence) aspects of speaking-up have been studied: the Core Collection of the Web of

Science yielded results for "employee silence" dated from 2003 until 2023, while for "Employee Voice" from 1972 until 2023. In terms of the body of research, the same database shows that although the number of results has steadily increased over the past 20 years, "employee silence" has yet to catch-up with "employee voice", and for example, for 2022 and 2021, 53 and 43 results were identified for "employee silence"; at the same time, 177 and 182 results were identified for "employee voice", respectively.

While positive leadership behaviors and supportive organizational cultures can significantly contribute to motivating productive behaviors at work, it would be unwise not to give equal attention to what motivates and maintains counterproductive work behaviors, toxic work environments and abusive leadership. From a practical point of view, interventions aimed at tackling problems in the workplace *via* strengthening "positive" aspects of work or the individual (e.g. mindfulness-based interventions for burnout) [3] have not yielded strong and/or long-lasting effects. However, it is not clear whether—to some extent—this happens due to the limitations of asymmetrical research and its inability to properly reflect the realities of both positive and negative dynamics. It is probably safe to assume that there are also significant knowledge gaps regarding the mechanisms that enable and maintain negative, counterproductive work behaviors that, actually contribute positively to both individual and organizational performance. As noted by Robert Hare, "If I wasn't studying psychopaths in prison, I'd do it in the stock exchange" [4].

Personality might be one of the most researched constructs in psychology, and more specifically, in organizational psychology, the research on the relationship between personality traits and several work and organization-related concepts is considerable. Personality traits have been examined in various ways, such as predicting variables [5], moderators [6, 7], and mediators [8]. More recently work-related models have been developed, suggesting that personality can also be influenced by work factors (e.g., Demands-Affordances Transactional "DATA" model) [9]. According to Heller et al. [10], when discussing personality with regard to work, approaches like the person-by-situation interaction approach to personality [11] and the role personality approach [12] can allow us to understand both the stability and variation of personality traits across situations and time. Further focusing on dark personality, the aforementioned approaches can be further enriched by introducing a functionalist approach to personality traits, which allows looking into the motives (e.g. goals or values), abilities (e.g. cognitive and psychological capacities) and perceptions (e.g. understandings of how the world works) [13]. In the field of organizational psychology, the dark personality traits—such as narcissism, Machiavellianism and psychopathy— have recently received increasing attention with respect to their diverse associations with work-related outcomes such as burnout [14, 15], elevated turnover rates [16], abusive leadership [17–19], employee silence [20], work-related motivation [21], resilience [22, 23], reduced job satisfaction [24], workplace behavior and organizational performance [25]. This chapter will review the existing evidence on how these dark traits are encountered and expressed in the workplace and propose directions for future research.

2. Dark personality traits and dark personalities

2.1 The dark triad and the dark tetrad

The first to coin the term "dark triad" were Paulhus and Williams [26] in an effort to link the personality traits of narcissism, Machiavellianism and psychopathy.

Callousness, manipulativeness and disagreeableness lie at the core of these three personality traits [27]. The dark triad (DT) is a structure of three theoretically distinct (though empirically overlapping) personality characteristics (psychopathy, Machiavellianism and narcissism) that are largely characterized by interpersonal maladaptation [28, 29] and fall under the umbrella of antagonism [30]. Psychopathy, as part of the DT, is characterized by a lack of conscience and guilt [31, 32], as well as uncooperative behavior in a variety of social situations [33, 34], and it has been suggested that lower levels of cooperativeness pay higher rewards for individuals scoring higher in psychopathy [35]. The second trait of the DT, Machiavellianism, is a psychological notion that was developed approximately between 1954 and 1955 and has been identified as the core of manipulation with four main characteristics: lack of emotional affection within interpersonal relationships, lack of interest in conventional morality, lack of psychopathology awareness and lack of ideological commitment [36]. The third trait of the DT is narcissism, a term first used by Havelock Ellis [37] to describe a clinical condition of auto-eroticism. Narcissism is a relatively constant differentiation of human personality characterized mainly by a sense of magnificence, overrated sensation of beauty and falsified views of oneself, extending to individual, interpersonal relationships and self-regulation strategies, as well as self-enhancement and social dominance [38, 39]. The DT (narcissism, Machiavellianism and psychopathy) has been recently expanded to include subclinical sadism [40, 41], leading to the development of the dark tetrad. Higher scores in sadism are linked to hurting others verbally, physically and psychologically and deriving pleasure from these actions [42].

The DT is sometimes discussed as the polar opposite of the so-called "Light Triad", which includes Kantianism (treating people as means to themselves—the opposite of Machiavellianism), Humanism (valuing the dignity and worth of each individual) and Faith in Humanity (believing in the fundamental goodness of humans) [43]. Moreover, the Honesty-Humility (HH) trait from the HEXACO personality inventory has also been added to the polar opposites of the DT with significant, high negative correlations between the two [30]. HH is associated with adjectives such as fair, generous and modest while being opposed to adjectives such as dishonest, unfair, greedy and boastful [44, 45]—all of which could describe DT traits—and is considered to be associated with altruism and/or cooperation *via* a reluctance to exploit others even when one could get away with doing it [46]. Differences in HH are associated with individual differences in the tendency to be authentic at the interpersonal level, to avoid deception and corruption, to not care about social status and wealth, to be humble and modest and to be willing to give up personal gain for collective benefit [46, 47].

In order to better understand the relationship between dark personality traits and work/organization-related outcomes, it is essential to take into account what is known about the "nature" of the so-called dark traits and "dark behaviors"—especially given that such behaviors can often be detected in leadership positions, constituting risk factors for both the well-being of employees and the organization as a whole [48]. While there are arguments supporting that some work-related behaviors are role-specific and not indicative of the person's personality traits, research evidence also shows that, for example, adopting a callous and manipulative attitude at work can also be a state of mind far beyond a role-restricted behavior. For example, Jonason & Zeigler-Hill [49] found that Machiavellianism and psychopathy were negatively associated with the desire to develop or maintain interpersonal relationships. Behaviors and attitudes that entail deprioritizing good relationships with others or an increased desire for status with complete disregard for others are potentially rooted in the primary experiences of social-ecological environments that reinforced individualistic self-preservation over collective prosperity—meaning that such behaviours and attitudes have been integrated over time in the "repertoire" of patterns that can be described as a person's personality, in this case, a dark personality.

From an evolutionary psychology perspective, humans, as social animals, have developed motives that serve their fundamental needs, including self-preservation, mate-seeking, status and kin care [50]. According to Jonason et al. [51], these social motives are sensitive to early experiences, especially stressful and unpredictable ones [52]. For example, experiences of unpredictability during childhood have been positively associated with higher levels of dark personality traits and status-seeking, while childhood resource availability has been negatively associated with the same traits [49]. These findings suggest the possibility of a "continuity" in the way the dark traits are developed and reinforced by the external environment. Moreover, if experienced as effective coping strategies for self-preservation and success, these behaviors and attitudes can be transferred to the work environment especially when found in organizational cultures where the focus on status overpowers the importance of interpersonal relationships. Thus, the interplay between work environments and dark personalities can be moderated and/or mediated by individual factors related to non-work and potentially to early life experiences as well.

2.2 Lack of empathy as the (missing) link across dark personality traits

One of the most agreed principles in the literature of dark personalities is the shared lack of empathy across the dark traits, which can also be expressed as a lack of concern for other people's welfare and/or a propensity to take advantage of them [53–56]. According to Wispé [57], empathy is conceptualized as the deliberate effort to consider others' emotions, and comprehend their ideas and perspectives to achieve interpersonal reciprocity. It is a vital and universal skill that is significant for co-existing in societies and moral development. Walker and Alligood [58] have suggested distinguishing between emotional (affective) and cognitive empathy. The latter is viewed as a taught skill, whereas the former is thought to be an intrinsic ability [58]; it is the lack of emotional empathy that is probably at the core of the dark personalities, as a large body of research has shown a systematic negative correlation between the dark personality traits and emotional empathy [59, 60]. A study by Turner et al. [61] suggested that the lowest levels of emotional empathy were identified among people with high levels of psychopathy, followed by those with higher levels of Machiavellianism and then narcissism. Interestingly—with the exception of psychopathy—this relationship was negative for emotional empathy with narcissism and Machiavellianism but positive for cognitive empathy with the same two traits. Furthermore, research indicated that those with greater levels of narcissism and Machiavellianism have the most robust cognitive empathy skill sets [61, 62]—which suggests that the ability to cognitively "put oneself in someone else's shoes" is probably distinct from the ability to emotionally relate to how someone else is feeling in a particular situation. High levels of cognitive empathy among individuals high in Machiavellianism and/or narcissism could potentially help explain what has often been described as an ability to emotionally manipulate others. Such manipulation is achieved by recognizing and understanding (cognitively) other's emotions and utilizing this to gain an advantage. Psychopathy, on the other hand, was not related to cognitive empathy, which may imply that those with high levels of psychopathy could be employing force or other manipulative techniques that rely less on cognitive empathy.

Recently, a novel psychological construct characterized by high empathy and dark traits has been proposed, the "dark empath" [63]. The term *dark empath* can be used to describe potentially "hidden" dark personalities, referring to individuals that are perceived as charming, who approach other people with warmth and attitudes that suggest care and concern; however, the aims are individualistic, and often the outcome is negative. The construct of the dark empath [63] could be used as an example of the combination between high cognitive empathy skills and high levels of Machiavellianism; this could be reminiscent of the well-known adage "the ends justify the means". Unlike emotional empathy, which is characterized by an innate desire to soothe the other person, in the case of the dark empath, there is no pleasure in helping other people; what matters is their personal goals that usually include achieving power and power assertion. We can imagine the aspect of learned (cognitive) empathy by people falling under the Dark Triad umbrella as an additional, dangerous and powerful tool used to achieve manipulation with precision. However, because these toxic behaviors and intentions are masked under the externally expressed cognitive empathy, it is hard to identify potentially "dangerous" individuals generally—but more specifically in the workplace.

3. Dark traits in the workplace: more complex than it seems?

3.1 Placing the dark traits in the workplace: OCB and WCB

Organizational citizenship behavior (OCB) can be used as a useful framework to better understand dark personality traits in the workplace. OCB describes a working environment where employees are internally motivated to go beyond duty and contribute to the organization without expecting a specific formal reward [63]. This type of engagement has been related to organizational benefits, such as increased job performance, less absenteeism and better organizational productivity [64]. On the other side of the scale lies counterproductive work behavior (CWB), which refers to behaviors that harm or intend to harm an organization or its employees [65].

According to Bennett and Robinson [66], CWB, or workplace deviance, a voluntary behavior intended to harm the organization and its members. These behaviors include sabotage, theft, or absenteeism and incivility, gossip or bullying (intended to hurt the organization's members). Research evidence has shown a positive and significant relationship between all dark traits and CWB in general [67, 68].

While dark personality traits have been found to be positively correlated with negative workplace behaviors [25], personality traits such as conscientiousness and agreeableness have been negatively correlated with CWB [69, 70] and positively correlated with OCB [71]. Thus, in an organizational context, the traits that comprise the dark triad and Tetrad are linked to CWB and antisocial tendencies in diverse work contexts. This highlights the urgency to review and further investigate the dark personality traits in the workplace, especially when considering people in leadership positions. It is also crucial to go one step back and explore the motives behind such behaviors, as these motives could constitute significant obstacles to well-being, job engagement and better performance in the workplace.

The risk of developing toxic work environments becomes greater when individuals scoring high on the dark personality traits are located in leadership positions, as the previously described motives and personal agendas have a huge toll on the employees' well-being. However, the alignment between the "job description" of a leadership position and the power motive that characterizes the dark personalities means that the probability of individuals with strong dark traits ending up in leadership role is—in many industries—high. McClelland [71] defined power motive as the desire to feel strong and make an impact on others, with the latter sustaining reputation and increasing prestige. Schattke & Marion-Jetten [72] suggest that power is an important motivator at work, and it is not necessarily attractive only to those scoring high on dark traits. However, it would be probably safe to hypothesize that higher levels of Machiavellianism, for example, would be correlated with greater efforts to achieve power, and often this means willingness to do "whatever it takes".

A strong desire for power and the need to dominate others play a significant role in dark leadership [48]. Suessenbach et al. [73] introduced a taxonomy of reasons for power desire. This derives from the assumption that individuals on the top of the social hierarchy obtain their power from three different sources: dominance, prestige and leadership. More specifically, dominance is based on forcing others to do something, and individuals with high motive for dominance force their will onto others by coercion and intimidation [73]. Prestige refers to the desire to seek admiration and respect while being on the top of the social hierarchy, and individuals with high motive for prestige seek voluntary deference through demonstrating their skills and knowledge. Leadership describes the situation in which someone takes responsibility for a group and directs its members towards a common goal. That position is obtained neither by force nor voluntary deference, but rather when the need for coordinating arises; individuals who enjoy directing others will try to acquire the leadership role [73]. However, the line between dominance and leadership seems to be very thin when it comes to dark personality traits, as an increased need for power and status might lead to counterproductive work behaviors and create a toxic environment for the rest of the employees. In fact, Schattke and Marion-Jetten [72] found that dominance was strongly associated with Machiavellianism while prestige was significantly related to narcissism. Furthermore, dominance predicted higher CWB, whereas leadership best predicted OCB. This could also help explain why narcissism—although included in the dark triad—is not always a "dark trait", with empirical evidence suggesting that when combined with high self-esteem narcissism is positively related to altruistic behaviour and intrinsic motivation for moral behaviour [74] and could also lead to "self-harming" altruistic behaviour, which has also been referred to as "pathological altruism" [75] or "extreme altruism" [76].

3.2 Dark traits and the well-being of colleagues, subordinates and/or supervisors: links with malevolent creativity

In the presence of dark personality traits in the workplace, apart from the employees' well-being and performance that might be affected, the organization is also at great risk for disloyalty and corruption. According to Harms et al. [77], dark personality traits are associated with antisocial and noxious interpersonal behaviors that could be used to predict inside threat behaviors. Moreover, both psychopathy and Machiavellianism predicted higher corruption intention [78], while narcissism was found to be unrelated to such outcomes. A longitudinal study by Nevicka et al. [79] showed that employees who interacted with leaders high on narcissistic traits encountered more toxic behaviors and regarded them as less effective in leadership.

Workplace bullying is conceptualized as a form of interpersonal misconduct in the workplace that involves repeated demeaning or destructive behaviors towards other organizational members [80]. Workplace bullying can be disruptive as it can cause psychological and physiological damage to the victims and negative work-related outcomes, such as job dissatisfaction and absenteeism [81]. Empirical evidence suggests that individuals with high levels of narcissism are more likely to use workplace bullying as a form of revenge when they do not get what they think they deserve [82]. This retaliation can take the form of spreading false rumors, social undermining, sabotage, bullying or harassment [82, 83].

Interestingly, the presence of narcissistic and psychopathic attributes in leaders has also been linked to workplace bullying, albeit indirectly, meaning that this group of leaders provides a suitable environment for the development and maintenance of workplace bullying [[84, 85] as cited in [86]]; thus, creating a toxic culture for the employees where disrespect, incivilities, and damage are tolerated or even indirectly rewarded. Machiavellianism and sadism have also been linked to workplace bullying, but the connection of the latter still remains primarily on a theoretical level with scarce research [[87] as cited in [86, 88, 89]]. Some evidence on sadism in connection to workplace bullying comes from Fernández-del-Río et al. [90], who found that all dark traits were related to workplace bullying, but sadism was the strongest predictor. This is in line with the conceptualization of sadists as people who derive pleasure from hurting others.

The dark traits have also been linked to workplace incivility [84, 91]. Incivility, according to Leiter et al. [92], is defined as rude or discourteous behaviors with somewhat ambiguous intent. Meier and Semmer [91] found that narcissism predicted incivility towards supervisors and coworkers. As narcissism is characterized by grandiosity, exhibitionism, and arrogance [83], rude behaviors towards supervisors can be explained by feelings of superiority and self-righteousness, meaning that they deserve the leadership position more than their supervisors. In relation to psychopathy, Boddy [84] found that high prevalence of psychopathy in a corporate setting was linked to increased rude behaviors, while Gebben et al. [93] provided some support for the positive links between sadism and uncivil behaviors in the workplace.

One interesting link between dark traits and CWB is malevolent creativity. Malevolent creativity can be defined as "creativity that is deliberately planned to damage others" (p. 106) [94]. In the workplace, malevolent creativity can range from gossip, lying, and cheating to verbal and physical abuse and fraud [95]. Kapoor and Kaufman [96] found that lower concerns for authority, loyalty, purity (binding moral foundations) and lower regard for care and fairness (individualizing moral foundations) predicted malevolent creativity. Congruently, the relationship between lower concerns for moral foundations and malevolent creativity was mediated by higher dark traits. For example, high narcissism allows individuals to engage in toxic and immoral behavior due to the antagonistic aspects that define this trait [67]. However, if we also consider that high levels of narcissism make it more likely to excel in certain tasks due to its adaptability [97], creativity can take the form of blame-shifting, gaslighting and revenge. For example, using any means necessary and, if needed, increasing levels of malevolent creativity to get what they think they deserve can be common behaviors that contribute to a hostile work environment with negative psychological and emotional consequences for coworkers, supervisors and/or subordinates.

Much less research has been published concerning psychopathy and malevolent creativity, but given the egocentricity that permeates psychopathy and characterizes psychopathic behavior, a link between psychopathy and malevolent creativity can be hypothesized. Higher levels of aggression are common among people with high levels of psychopathy (e.g. the "Corporate Psychopath"), as are immoral behavior and malevolent thinking [98], and, combined with the high levels of deception and lying [99], psychopathy could lead to greater levels of malevolent creativity. However, research has also challenged the idea that psychopaths are better at lying and deceiving [100, 101], thus making it difficult to draw direct conclusions between psychopathy and malevolent creativity. On the other hand, there is support for a positive relationship between psychopathy and malevolent divergent thinking that could be attributed to the hypothesis that certain personality characteristics predispose individuals to certain actions [102, 103].

Malevolent creativity is also more common among individuals with a "Machiavellian" profile [104, 105]. Examples of malevolent creativity, include generating lies, daydreaming about hurting people, planning pranks and the willingness to commit fraud [23, 106, 107]. Lastly, bullying and sensation-seeking appear to be the most common expression of malevolent creativity among individuals with high levels of sadism [40, 108]. The first includes threats of violence, the use of fear tactics, trolling, cyberstalking and doxing [95, 109], while the latter refers to the tendency to pursue new and different sensations, feelings and experiences, often at the expense of other people, with significant risks for the well-being of an organization.

3.3 The case of "corporate psychopathy"

Psychopathy is a term identified in clinical psychopathology which refers to a pattern of behaviors identified under the antisocial personality disorder (ASPD) in DSM-5 [110], classified with two severe personality disorders—Borderline (BPD) and Narcissistic (NPD) personality disorder. Psychopathy has been defined as "a mental disorder roughly equivalent to antisocial personality disorder, but with an emphasis on affective and interpersonal traits such as superficial charm, pathological lying, egocentricity, lack of remorse, and callousness" [111]. ASPD is described as a personality disorder characterized by a rigidly dysfunctional thought process with a significant focus on "social irresponsibility" or even "social injustice", combined with delinquent, exploitive and criminal behaviors. The lack of remorse is at the core of the disorder, even in cases of severe criminal activity with potential physical and mental harm to others. According to the DSM-5 [110], diagnostic criteria for ASPD include a pervasive pattern of disregard and violation of the rights of others, with significant impairments in self-functioning and interpersonal functioning, while pathological personality traits should be identified in the domains of Antagonism and Disinhibition.

The term "Corporate Psychopathy" has been directly associated with the notion of "dark personality" and its related traits [112]. Individuals who fall under the "Corporate Psychopathy" label work in corporations and other business organizations and have been often described as careerists, charming, manipulative, cunning and opportunistic but with fast-track careers in business organizations [112]. Corporate Psychopathy fulfills "Antagonism" and "Disinhibition" criteria of psychopathy by exhibiting manipulativeness, deceitfulness, callousness and hostility (for Antagonism) and irresponsibility, impulsivity and risk-taking (for Disinhibition); characteristics that are reflective of what could be described as dishonest and immoral behavior. It is crucial to underline that Corporate Psychopathy pertains to behaviors displayed in the work context, whereas ASPD involves impairments in personality functioning and trait expression, that remain relatively stable across time. In essence, Corporate Psychopathy is associated with an individual's role-based personality, while ASPD is linked to their overall/global personality and situations. A relevant question worth exploring is, what underlying mechanism might contribute to these types of behaviors.

To better understand the potential mechanisms, the cognitive toolbox of "Corporate Psychopathy", and, more specifically, the role of cognitive control, could be a useful pathway. Cognitive control refers to one's ability to guide their own behavior, thoughts and emotions [113]. Although a matter of a long-lasting and still ongoing debate, limited cognitive control [114, 115] is suggested to have an inverse relationship with dishonesty. The cognitive control network is comprised of three brain areas: (1) anterior cingulate cortex, (2) ventrolateral prefrontal cortex and (3) dorsolateral prefrontal cortex. Activity in the cognitive control neural network (as shown by fMRI studies) has been related to hindering automated selfish impulses [116]. Interestingly, a study with incarcerated individuals in the highest percentiles of psychopathy (often referred to as "psychopaths") revealed diminished activity of the cognitive control network when faced with an opportunity to exhibit dishonest behavior [117], suggesting that dishonesty may result from a lack of inhibition due to reduced activity of the cognitive control brain network. Similarly, disruption in this network has been linked to selfish impulses [118]. To our knowledge, the literature on the neurobiological substrates of "Corporate Psychopathy" is rather limited; however, the results on psychopathy, impulsivity and selfishness suggest that certain neurobiological substrates underly dishonest behavior. Thus, we should keep in mind the neurobiological mechanisms when exploring the role of personality traits in behavior. The neuronal networks that form the basis of personality can lead us towards a better understanding of explicit behavior and can provide further and valuable information on how these mechanisms can be altered in relation to one's environment, such as the working environment. Indeed, the importance of these neural networks becomes apparent when we consider the interplays between brain functioning and environmental circumstances, which ultimately affect the end result, that is, behavior; for a review, see [119].

One lay theory, based on the key tenets of evolutionary psychology, that aims to answer what makes a person turn (dis)honest the Will Hypothesis—where Will refers to the willpower needed to be honest [120]. The Will Hypothesis argues that people are inherently selfish and immoral and try to obtain gains (e.g. financial). In order for someone to be honest and moral, they need to exert cognitive control in order to inhibit these selfish and greedy behaviors. Evidence from cognitive psychology appear to corroborate the Will Hypothesis. Specifically, diminishing participants' ability for cognitive control (e.g. sleep deprivation, under time pressure and anxiety) makes them more likely to be dishonest [121–123].

From a work-personality perspective, when Corporate Psychopaths are found in supervisory positions, they are expected to exhibit abusive behaviors towards their subordinates. Abusive supervisor behaviors have been defined as "the sustained display of hostile verbal and nonverbal behaviors, excluding physical contact" (p. 178) [124] from a supervisor towards their subordinate(s) and are a form of CWB [112]. Abusive supervisor behaviors have been associated with higher scores in psychopathy [112]. Examples of abusive supervisor behaviors might include manipulation tactics, aggression, social dominance orientation, the pursuit of self-interests no matter the costs, bullying behaviour, etc.; these behaviors and qualities are extremely similar to the main descriptors of corporate psychopathy presented earlier. Such a profile very often fits with descriptions of abusive supervisors, toxic leaders, tyrant leaders, negative leaders, etc., with a negative impact on the well-being of coworkers and subordinates and the organization as a whole (**Figure 1**).

3.4 The well-being of the dark personalities

Apart from the relationship between abusive supervision/toxic leadership and the dark traits—where findings seem to consistently suggest that individuals who score higher in the dark triad, are more likely to exhibit abusive supervision and toxic

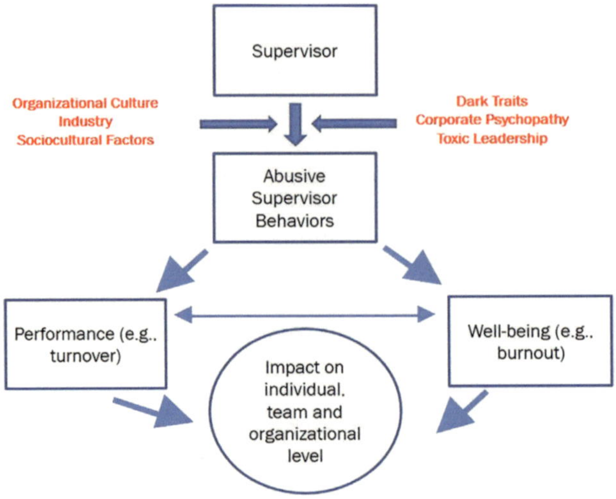

Figure 1.
The impact of abusive supervisor behaviors.

leadership behaviours—research findings have highlighted that the way the dark traits interact with other aspects of work life, such as burnout and collaboration, is complex and conditional.

For example, on a neurobiological note, burnout has been associated with diminished prefrontal cortex and anterior cingulate cortex activity, that is, the cognitive control network; for a review, see [125]. Thus, burnout could result in more dishonest toxic and impulsive behaviors in those employees who fall within the spectrum of the dark triad, meaning that high levels of burnout can "empower" CWBs in individuals scoring high in the dark traits.

Another example of the complex relationships surrounding the well-being of individuals scoring high on dark personality traits is that of motivation. A more nuanced analysis of the complex interplay between personality traits and work-related outcomes shows that despite their "dark" cluster of personalities, a recent study conducted by Szabó and colleagues [78] found that the association between the dark triad personality traits and work motivation (positive work-related aspect) varies depending on the specific dark trait. Narcissism was positively associated with intrinsic forms of work motivation, whereas psychopathy and Machiavellianism were linked to extrinsic forms of work motivation. In addition, the latter two traits were also related to a lack of motivation/amotivation.

Empirical evidence suggests that, people who score high on the dark traits typically have negative attitudes towards their jobs. The majority of studies have found a negative correlation between dark triad traits and organizational commitment [126, 127] as well as job satisfaction [128, 129]. These results support the hypothesis that the dark triad is linked to poor work attitudes. It is important to highlight that these relationships are not consistent across the different dark traits. For instance, Galvin et al. [130] reported that people with high levels of narcissism not only had a strong sense of affiliation with the organization but also thought of themselves as being essential to its identity.

The very ambiguous nature of the dark traits has resulted in research leaning towards confirming that dark traits are "bad news" for everyone else, which means that the empirical evidence is unbalanced. The available evidence suggests that perspective-taking is an important issue when examining the well-being associated with dark traits. For example, CWBs might be experienced positively by individuals scoring high on certain dark traits - meaning that for some, higher well-being can be a byproduct of others misery. Thus, the association between dark traits and work-related outcomes can negatively and positively influence the workplace, depending on the perspective taken. For example, while narcissism may be positively associated with achievement motivation and job satisfaction, it can also lead to interpersonal conflicts and toxic work environments [131].

3.5 Does dark personality help individuals get ahead at work?

The evidence on the negative consequences of toxic leadership and abusive supervision for employee-well-being is ample. However, anecdotal evidence suggests that individuals who score high on dark personality traits can be found in managerial positions, and might be more likely to get promoted. Moreover, abusive and toxic leadership is still tolerated in most industries and aspects of toxic organizational culture are maintained over time (e.g., bullying, employee silence). The belief that dark personality helps us get ahead at work is very common, from the great political scene to local businesses. Several headlines about scandals revealing "dark aspects" of successful professional people might have also strengthened this public opinion [132].

Some empirical evidence suggests that specific dark traits are positively associated with job performance. For example, Fernández-del-Río et al. [88] found that narcissism and Machiavellianism were positive predictors of task performance, while only the former was positively correlated with contextual performance. Psychopathy and sadism were negative predictors of task performance, while sadism was positively related to CWB. While the limitations of quantitative research restrict these findings, it would be reasonable to hypothesize that in work environments where task performance is valorized, high levels of narcissism and/or Machiavellianism could be considered a "competitive advantage".

Along with task performance, political skill has become one of the most desirable qualities in several industries, especially in higher-level positions. Political skill has been suggested as a potential pathway to explain why individuals who possess darker personality traits might be able to get ahead at work more easily sometimes. Political skills are connected to several favorable professional results and career benefits. A study conducted by Templer [133] measured the Honesty-Humility (HH) trait from the HEXACO personality taxonomy to assess whether individuals who score low on HH are more likely to get ahead at work. As mentioned earlier, HH has been found to have a strong negative correlation to dark personality traits such as the dark triad [134] and could be considered a conceptual opposite of dark personality. Templer [133] identified that—although there was a positive direct relationship between HH and performance—the indirect effect was of the opposite direction: the least honest-humble employees were more likely to perceive themselves as the more politically skilled. When their supervisors also view them as politically skilled, their work performance will be rated higher; given that performance rating is crucial for promotion and professional advancement, it is possible that in jobs and professions where political skill is highly valued, employees scoring higher on the dark traits might have an advantage against the more honest-humble ones. Those that score high on political skills understand how to promote themselves and influence others while pretending to have no hidden motivations [133]. This can also be linked to the previously discussed relationships between dark traits and cognitive empathy.

This leads us to hypothesize that the dark traits might be linked to impression management—with impression management tactics positively linked to certain career and professional outcomes such as job interviews and job performance [135].

For example, humor is often used as a mechanism for impression management in the workplace, and Torres-Marín et al. [136] found distinct characteristics in humor styles, disposition towards ridicule and laughter, and comic styles among the dark traits. Narcissism was the only dark trait linked to "lighter" forms of humor relating to the formation of social and emotional bonds with others, having no problem being laughed at and even enjoying it and using affiliative humor, fun and wit. This behavior can be explained by narcissists' disposition to draw attention to themselves [26, 137]. Psychopathy was linked to "darker" forms of humor, including aggressive humor, joy in laughing at the expense of others and sarcasm. Psychopaths are characterized by high degrees of inventiveness and an inability for self-control [56], possibly serving as an explanation for their humor-related personality systems [136]. Machiavellianism was only linked to an increased fear of being laughed at and the use of an ironic/satiric comic style. The necessity to preserve their reputation [56] could explain the ironic/satiric comic style, which could also serve as a defense mechanism against the fear of being laughed at. At the same time, this interaction reveals their disposition for manipulativeness and their ability to create schemes to achieve their goals. Lastly, sadism was linked to aggressive humor, sarcasm and the joy of laughing at the expense of others. Humor also dovetails with the previously discussed concept of malevolent creativity. Overall, dark traits are linked to increasingly more complex, imaginative and creative ways to harm others for personal gain or amusement—humour could be one pathway to success. Humor can mask several negative behaviors, including blame-shifting, gaslighting, revenge, deception, lying, planning malevolent pranks, threats of violence, use of fear tactics, trolling, cyberstalking, doxing and fraud. Apart from the negative effects that such behaviors have on the well-being of others, in work environments where competitiveness is promoted and where the achievement of organizational goals is not aligned with the well-being of the employees, the ability to trick or harm others using sophisticated schemes is often considered an asset and is highly valorized. Thus, in cultures where such qualities are valued, "dark personalities" are more likely to be rewarded by getting ahead.

The ability to adapt and adjust to an organization's culture has been proposed as a potential link between career outcomes and certain dark traits, particularly in relation to resilience in non-supportive and highly competitive environments. Bereczkei [138] suggests that dark traits allow individuals to modify their behavior according to their surroundings or organizational contexts, which may include factors such as organizational culture, leadership style, and perceived organizational politics [139, 140]. Moreover, another line of research has explored the role of perceived organizational support in mitigating the negative effects of dark traits among employees. In their study, Palmer and colleagues [141] revealed that employees with high levels of narcissism and psychopathy were less likely to engage in certain forms of counterproductive work behavior when they perceived their organization as supportive. Specifically, Choi [142] provided additional support by demonstrating that perceived organizational support mitigated the adverse impact of employee narcissism on work satisfaction.

It is important to highlight, however, that this is not evidence of causality, meaning that there is no substantial proof that dark traits are a *cause* of career/professional success, even if some research has shown that dark traits strongly predict better pay and leadership positions [143] among early-career employees. What we can conclude, though, is that this is an indication of what types of behaviors and attitudes are valued in a workplace and what it says for organizational cultures. Cultures that are only interested in success and gains above all else are more likely to tolerate and even reward behaviors that belong in the dark personalities' repertoire. For example, the need to ensure that a person in a senior leadership position can make a difficult decision might nudge towards hiring someone less driven by empathy and more driven by the "the ends justifying the needs"-approach. Thus, firing subordinates or colleagues might come with a big toll for more empathetic persons whose personal values do not align with the objective financial goals of an organization; but it might be emotionally easier for a more "Machiavellian" personality. However, while there might be certain benefits for the organization, it remains difficult to estimate whether the benefits are more than the losses, given the effects of "dark leaders" on the well-being of subordinates and coworkers [144]. Of course, there are also examples were whole organizations collapsed. We can refer to Nick Leeson [145], a young trader who received early approval to conduct financial transactions on behalf of his bank and made fraudulent and illegal decisions. The oldest commercial bank in the United Kingdom, Barings Bank, collapsed directly due to his acts.

4. Implications

4.1 Practical implications for leadership and organizational management

Dark traits are often present in high positions at work, producing CWB, limiting job engagement, job performance and well-being. Therefore, addressing the issue from within and understanding the motives can provide important insights into such behaviors. Detecting and assessing dark personality traits in the workplace can contribute to constructing interventions and policies that restrict toxic behaviors and promote general well-being and intrinsic motivation to work. This will lead to a better work climate, better job performance and higher productivity. Furthermore, the organization itself can benefit by re-examining inside threats, disloyalty and corruption intentions.

The evidence concerning the dark traits in the workplace presents an interesting challenge for leaders and managers. For example, are "dark personalities" a necessary evil in a capitalist environment? Put more simply, is the ubiquitous need to "get things done" across all industries the driving force behind the impetus for the ends to always justify the means?

4.2 Implications for research

The "traditional" issues related to measuring personality constructs remain and still need to be better addressed; social desirability bias is expected to be more common when measuring constructs that are negatively regarded, meaning that individuals high on dark traits are more likely to deceive and lie. However, it is also important to acknowledge that the relationship between dark personality traits and negative outcomes is not always straightforward, and other factors may influence how these traits are expressed in the job context.

Furthermore, it should be emphasized that despite extensive research and scholarly attention directed towards the dark triad [26], many critical queries about this construct have yet to be resolved. In particular, the absence of a distinct and precise definition of the construct of dark personalities has hindered progress and resulted in inconsistent descriptions of their empirical profile. Specifically, there is a lack of a commonly accepted and unified definition of the dark triad, as noted by Crowe et al. [146], who stated that "a consensual definition of the construct is still lacking" (p. 1).

Moreover, there is a significant research gap in terms of the positive aspects of dark traits in the workplace. For example, Volmer et al. [147] found that leaders exhibiting high levels of narcissism can enhance their subordinates' perceived levels of career success and satisfaction without impinging upon their well-being. There is a significant gap in the literature, as existing studies have primarily focused on negative outcomes associated with dark personality traits. The lack of attention to positive outcomes is a notable oversight, as it fails to capture the nuanced and complex nature of how dark personality traits operate in the workplace. Additionally, understanding the potential positive outcomes associated with dark personality traits is essential for developing strategies to leverage these traits to benefit both the individual and the organization.

Future research needs to consider the bidirectional association of this relationship, as it is possible that certain industries or professions may be more conducive to the expression and maintenance of dark personality traits, thereby leading to self-selection processes in which individuals with higher levels of dark traits are drawn to and excel in such contexts [51, 147, 148]. Thus, there is reason to explore the possibility of a feedback loop.

5. Summary of main points

While individuals arrive in the workplace with pre-developed personalities and predispositions, it is possible in certain occupations or industries, dark traits are reinforced and even rewarded as a result of occupational socialization, training and promotion within these work environments. Future research should focus on identifying and understanding the four distinct types of effects, namely nonlinear, interactive, differential and reciprocal, that highlight the multifaceted nature of these traits in the context of organizations to allow for practical implications that can help minimize the harm and use benefits of darkness for a lighter, brighter work environment, leading to what might be called the *good Machiavelli*.

Conflict of interest

The authors declare no conflict of interest.

Author details

Olga Lainidi[1*], Vilma Chalili[2], Ilias Maliousis[2], Maria Spiliou[2], Eva Tzioti[2], Panagiota Koutsimani[3] and Anthony Montgomery[4]

1 School of Psychology, University of Leeds, UK

2 School of Psychology, Mediterranean College Thessaloniki Campus, Greece

3 Department of Psychology, School of Social Sciences and Humanities, University of Western Macedonia, Greece

4 Department of Psychology, Northumbria University, UK

*Address all correspondence to: o.lainidi@leeds.ac.uk

References

[1] Schyns B. Dark personality in the workplace: Introduction to the special issue. Applied Psychology. 2015;**64**(1):1-4

[2] Morrison EW. Employee voice and silence: Taking stock a decade later. Annual Review of Organizational Psychology and Organizational Behavior. 2023;**10**(1):79-107

[3] Bartlett L, Martin A, Neil AL, Memish K, Otahal P, Kilpatrick M, et al. A systematic review and meta-analysis of workplace mindfulness training randomized controlled trials. Journal of Occupational Health Psychology. 2019 Feb;**24**(1):108

[4] Hare RD. Without Conscience: The Disturbing World of the Psychopaths among us. New York City: Guilford Press; 1999

[5] Armon G, Shirom A, Melamed S. The big five personality factors as predictors of changes across time in burnout and its facets. Journal of Personality. 2012;**80**(2):403-427

[6] Parkes KR. Personality and coping as moderators of work stress processes: Models, methods and measures. Work & Stress. 1994;**8**(2):110-129

[7] Bowling NA, Eschleman KJ. Employee personality as a moderator of the relationships between work stressors and counterproductive work behavior. Journal of Occupational Health Psychology. 2010;**15**(1):91

[8] Singh AK, Singh S. Perceived organisational support and organisational citizenship behaviour: The mediating role of personality. Journal of the Indian Academy of Applied Psychology. 2013;**39**(1):117-125

[9] Woods SA, Wille B, Wu CH, Lievens F, De Fruyt F. The influence of work on personality trait development: The demands-affordances transactional (DATA) model, an integrative review, and research agenda. Journal of Vocational Behavior. 2019;**110**:258-271

[10] Heller D, Ferris DL, Brown D, Watson D. The influence of work personality on job satisfaction: Incremental validity and mediation effects. Journal of Personality. 2009;**77**(4):1051-1084

[11] Mischel W, Shoda Y. Reconciling processing dynamics and personality dispositions. Annual Review of Psychology. 1998;**49**(1):229-258

[12] Sheldon KM, Ryan RM, Rawsthorne LJ, Ilardi B. Trait self and true self: Cross-role variation in the big-five personality traits and its relations with psychological authenticity and subjective well-being. Journal of Personality and Social Psychology. 1997;**73**(6):1380

[13] Spain SM, Harms P, LeBreton JM. The dark side of personality at work. Journal of Organizational Behavior. 2014;**35**(S1):S41-S60

[14] Mirkovic D, Bianchi R. An exploratory study of the link between Machiavellianism and burnout. Personality and Individual Differences. 2019;**148**:27-31. DOI: 10.1016/j.paid.2019.05.024

[15] Čopková R. Burnout syndrome and dark triad at schools: Engineers as teachers of vocational technical subjects. Journal on Efficiency and Responsibility in Education and Science. 2021;**14**(3):195-203. DOI: 10.7160/eriesj.2021.140306

[16] Martinko MJ, Harvey P, Brees JR, Mackey J. A review of abusive supervision research. Journal of Organizational Behavior. 2013;**34**(S1):S120-S137. DOI: 10.1002/job.1888

[17] Hogan R, Kaiser RB, Sherman RA, Harms PD. Twenty years on the dark side: Six lessons about bad leadership. Consulting Psychology Journal: Practice and Research. 2021;**73**(3):199-213. DOI: 10.1037/cpb0000205

[18] Khan AN, Khan NA, Bodla AA, Gul S. Impact of psychopathy on employee creativity via work engagement and negative socioemotional behavior in public health sector. Personnel Review. 2020;**49**(8):1655-1675. DOI: 10.1108/pr-02-2019-0072

[19] Hogan R, Hogan J. Assessing leadership: A view from the dark side. International Journal of Selection and Assessment. 2001;**9**(1 & 2):40-51. DOI: 10.1111/1468-2389.00162

[20] Hamstra MRW, Schreurs B, Jawahar IMJ, Laurijssen LM, Hünermund P. Manager narcissism and employee silence: A socio-analytic theory perspective. Journal of Occupational and Organizational Psychology. 2021;**94**(1):29-54. DOI: 10.1111/joop.12337

[21] Szabó ZP, Diller SJ, Czibor A, Restás P, Jonas E, Frey D. "One of these things is not like the others": The associations between dark triad personality traits, work attitudes, and work-related motivation. Personality and Individual Differences. 2023;**205**:112098. DOI: 10.1016/j.paid.2023.112098

[22] Papageorgiou KA, Gianniou FM, Wilson P, Moneta GB, Bilello D, Clough PJ. The bright side of dark: Exploring the positive effect of narcissism on perceived stress through mental toughness. Personality and Individual Differences. 2019;**139**:116-124. DOI: 10.1016/j.paid.2018.11.004

[23] Szabó E, Körmendi A, Kurucz G, Cropley D, Olajos T, Pataky N. Personality traits as predictors of malevolent creative ideation in offenders. Behavioral Sciences. 2022;**12**(7):242. DOI: 10.3390/bs12070242

[24] Jonason PK, Koenig BL, Tost J. Living a fast life. Human Nature. 2010;**21**(4):428-442. DOI: 10.1007/s12110-010-9102-4

[25] O'Boyle EH, Forsyth DR, Banks GC, McDaniel MA. A meta-analysis of the dark triad and work behavior: A social exchange perspective. Journal of Applied Psychology. 2012;**97**(3):557-579. DOI: 10.1037/a0025679

[26] Paulhus DL, Williams KM. The dark triad of personality: Narcissism, Machiavellianism, and psychopathy. Journal of Research in Personality. 2002;**36**(6):556-563. DOI: 10.1016/s0092-6566(02)00505-6

[27] Marcus DK, Preszler J, Zeigler-Hill V. A network of dark personality traits: What lies at the heart of darkness? Journal of Research in Personality. 2018;**73**:56-62. DOI: 10.1016/j.jrp.2017.11.003

[28] Furnham A, Richards SC, Paulhus DL. The dark triad of personality: A 10 year review. Social and Personality Psychology Compass. 2013;**7**:199-216

[29] Fehr B, Samsom D. The construct of Machiavellianism: Twenty years later. Advances in Personality Assessment. 2013;**9**:77

[30] Vize CE, Collison KL, Miller JD, Lynam DR. The "core" of the dark triad: A test of competing hypotheses.

Personality Disorders: Theory, Research, and Treatment. 2020;**11**:91

[31] Hare RD, Neumann CS. Psychopathy as a clinical and empirical construct. Annual Review of Clinical Psychology. 2008;**4**:217-246

[32] Giannini F, Raimondi R. Psychopathological excursus on anti-social personality disorder, psychopathy and the dark triad: A review of international literature. Journal of Psychopathology. 2020;**26**:242-247

[33] Babiak P, Hare RD, McLaren T. Snakes in suits: When psychopaths go to work. New York: Harper, 2007

[34] Baggio MC, Benning SD. The influence of psychopathic traits and strategic harshness on point gain and cooperation rate in the Prisoner's dilemma. Personality and Individual Differences. 2022;**186**:111344

[35] Harris GT, Rice ME. Treatment of psychopathy. In: Patrick CJ, editor. Handbook of Psychopathy. New York, NY, USA: The Guilford Press; 2006. pp. 555-572

[36] Stenason L, Vernon PA. The dark triad, reinforcement sensitivity and substance use. Personality and Individual Differences. 2016;**94**:59-63

[37] Ellis H. Auto-erotism: A psychological study. Alienist and Neurologist (1880-1920). 1898;**19**:260

[38] Campbell WK, Hoffman BJ, Campbell SM, Marchisio G. Narcissism in organizational contexts. Human Resource Management Review. 2011;**21**:268-284

[39] Nenadić I, Lorenz C, Gaser C. Narcissistic personality traits and prefrontal brain structure. Scientific Reports. 2021;**11**:15707

[40] Chabrol H, Van Leeuwen N, Rodgers R, Séjourné N. Contributions of psychopathic, narcissistic, Machiavellian, and sadistic personality traits to juvenile delinquency. Personality and Individual Differences. 2009;**47**(7):734-739. DOI: 10.1016/j.paid.2009.06.020

[41] Paulhus DL. Toward a taxonomy of dark personalities. Current Directions in Psychological Science. 2014;**23**(6):421-426. DOI: 10.1177/0963721414547737

[42] Buckels EE, Jones DN, Paulhus DL. Behavioral confirmation of everyday sadism. Psychological Science. 2013;**24**(11):2201-2209. DOI: 10.1177/0956797613490749

[43] Kaufman SB, Yaden DB, Hyde E, Tsukayama E. The light vs. dark triad of personality: Contrasting two very different profiles of human nature. Frontiers in Psychology. 2019;**10**:467

[44] Ashton MC, Lee K, Goldberg LR. The IPIP–HEXACO scales: An alternative, public-domain measure of the personality constructs in the HEXACO model. Personality and Individual Differences. 2007;**42**:1515-1526

[45] Ashton MC, Lee K. On the relations between HEXACO agreeableness (versus anger) and honesty-humility. Scandinavian Journal of Psychology. 2021;**62**:887-894

[46] De Vries RE, van Kampen D. The HEXACO and 5DPT models of personality: A comparison and their relationships with psychopathy, egoism, pretentiousness, immorality, and Machiavellianism. Journal of Personality Disorders. 2010;**24**(2):244-257

[47] Columbus S. Honesty-humility, beliefs, and prosocial behaviour: A test on stockpiling during the COVID-19 pandemic. Collabra: Psychology. 2021;**7**(1):19028

[48] Furtner MR, Maran T, Rauthmann JF. Dark leadership: The role of leaders' dark triad personality traits. In: Clark MG, Gruber CW, editors. Leader Development Deconstructed. Springer; 2017. pp. 75-99

[49] Jonason PK, Zeigler-Hill V. The fundamental social motives that characterize dark personality traits. Personality and Individual Differences. 2018;**132**:98-107. DOI: 10.1016/j.paid.2018.05.031

[50] Neel R, Kenrick DT, White AJP, Neuberg SL. Individual differences in fundamental social motives. Journal of Personality and Social Psychology. 2016;**110**(6):887-907. DOI: 10.1037/pspp0000068

[51] Jonason PK, Icho A, Ireland K. Resources, harshness, and unpredictability. Evolutionary Psychology. 2016;**14**(1):147470491562369. DOI: 10.1177/1474704915623699

[52] Brumbach BH, Figueredo AJ, Ellis BJ. Effects of harsh and unpredictable environments in adolescence on development of life history strategies. Human Nature. 2009;**20**(1):25-51. DOI: 10.1007/s12110-009-9059-3

[53] Heym N, Firth J, Kibowski F, Sumich A, Egan V, Bloxsom CA. Empathy at the heart of darkness: Empathy deficits that bind the dark triad and those that mediate indirect relational aggression. Frontiers in Psychiatry. 2019;**10**:95

[54] Szabó E, Bereczkei T. Different paths to different strategies? Unique associations among facets of the dark triad, empathy, and trait emotional intelligence. Advances in Cognitive Psychology. 2017;**13**(4):306

[55] Jones DN, Figueredo AJ. The core of darkness: Uncovering the heart of the dark triad. European Journal of Personality. 2013;**27**(6):521-531

[56] Jones DN, Paulhus DL. Introducing the short dark triad (SD3). Assessment. 2013;**21**(1):28-41. DOI: 10.1177/1073191113514105

[57] Wispé L. The distinction between sympathy and empathy: To call forth a concept, a word is needed. Journal of Personality and Social Psychology. 1986;**50**(2):314-321

[58] Walker KM, Alligood MR. Empathy from a nursing perspective: Moving beyond borrowed theory. Archives of Psychiatric Nursing. 2001;**15**(3):140-147

[59] Pajevic M, Vukosavljevic-Gvozden T, Stevanovic N, Neumann CS. The relationship between the dark tetrad and a two-dimensional view of empathy. Personality and Individual Differences. 2018;**123**:125-130. DOI: 10.1016/j.paid.2017.11.009

[60] Kajonius PJ, Björkman T. Individuals with dark traits have the ability but not the disposition to empathize. Personality and Individual Differences. 2020;**155**:109716

[61] Turner IN, Foster JD, Webster GD. The dark Triad's inverse relations with cognitive and emotional empathy: High-powered tests with multiple measures. Personality and Individual Differences. 2019;**139**:1-6

[62] Vonk J, Zeigler-Hill V, Mayhew P, Mercer S. Mirror mirror on the wall, which form of narcissist know self and others best of all. Personality and Individual Differences. 2013;**54**:396-401

[63] Heym N, et al. The dark empath: Characterising dark traits in the presence of empathy. Personality and Individual Differences. 2021;**169**:110172

[64] Organ DW. Organizational Citizenship Behavior: The Good Soldier

Syndrome. Lexington, Massachusetts: Lexington Books/DC Heath and Com; 1988

[65] Podsakoff NP, Whiting SW, Podsakoff PM, Blume BD. Individual- and organizational-level consequences of organizational citizenship behaviors: A meta-analysis. Journal of Applied Psychology. 2009;**94**(1):122

[66] Spector PE, Fox S. The stressor-emotion model of counterproductive work behavior. In: Counterproductive Work Behavior: Investigations of Actors and Targets. Washington, D.C., U.S.: American Psychological Association; 2005. pp. 151-174. DOI: 10.1037/10893-007

[67] Bennett RJ, Robinson SL. Development of a measure of workplace deviance. Journal of Applied Psychology. 2000;**85**(3):349-360. DOI: 10.1037/0021-9010.85.3.349

[68] Li C, Murad M, Shahzad F, Khan MA, Ashraf SF. Dark tetrad personality traits and counterproductive work behavior among doctors in Pakistan. The International Journal of Health Planning and Management. 2020;**35**(5):1173-1192

[69] Forsyth DR, Banks GC, McDaniel MA. A meta-analysis of the dark triad and work behavior: A social exchange perspective. Journal of Applied Psychology. 2012;**97**(3):557

[70] Runge JM, Lang JW, Zettler I, Lievens F. Predicting counterproductive work behavior: Do implicit motives have incremental validity beyond explicit traits? Journal of Research in Personality. 2020;**89**:104019. DOI: 10.1016/j.jrp.2020.104019

[71] Webster BD, Smith MB. The dark triad and organizational citizenship behaviors: The moderating role of high involvement management climate. Journal of Business and Psychology. 2018;**34**(5):621-635. DOI: 10.1007/s10869-018-9562-9

[72] McClelland DC. Power: The Inner Experience. Irvington: Halsted Press; 1975

[73] Schattke K, Marion-Jetten AS. Distinguishing the explicit power motives. Zeitschrift für Psychologie. 2022;**230**(4):290-299. DOI: 10.1027/2151-2604/a000481

[74] Suessenbach F, Loughnan S, Schönbrodt FD, Moore AB. The dominance, prestige, and leadership account of social power motives. European Journal of Personality. 2019;**33**(1):7-33. DOI: 10.1002/per.2184

[75] Hart W, Tortoriello GK, Richardson K. Feeling good about oneself heightens, not hinders, the goodness in narcissism. Current Psychology. 2019;**38**:1399-1408

[76] Kaufman SB, Jauk E. Healthy selfishness and pathological altruism: Measuring two paradoxical forms of selfishness. Frontiers in Psychology. 2020;**11**:1006

[77] White D, Szabo M, Tiliopoulos N. Exploring the relationship between narcissism and extreme altruism. American Journal of Psychology. 2018;**131**(1):65-80

[78] Harms P, Marbut A, Johnston AC, Lester P, Fezzey T. Exposing the darkness within: A review of dark personality traits, models, and measures and their relationship to insider threats. Journal of Information Security and Applications. 2022;**71**:103378. DOI: 10.1016/j.jisa.2022.103378

[79] Szabó ZP, Simon E, Czibor A, Restás P, Bereczkei T. The importance of dark personality traits in predicting

workplace outcomes. Personality and Individual Differences. 2021;**183**:111112. DOI: 10.1016/j.paid.2021.111112

[80] Nevicka B, De Hoogh AHB, Den Hartog DN, Belschak FD. Narcissistic leaders and their victims: Followers low on self-esteem and low on core self-evaluations suffer most. Frontiers in Psychology. 2018;**9**:422. DOI: 10.3389/fpsyg.2018.00422

[81] Rai A, Agarwal UA. Workplace bullying and employee silence: A moderated mediation model of psychological contract violation and workplace friendship. Personnel Review. 2018;**47**(1):226-256

[82] Samnani AK, Singh P. Workplace bullying: Considering the interaction between individual and work environment. Journal of Business Ethics. 2015;**139**(3):537-549. DOI: 10.1007/s10551-015-2653-x

[83] Perchtold-Stefan CM, Fink A, Rominger C, Papousek I. Failure to reappraise: Malevolent creativity is linked to revenge ideation and impaired reappraisal inventiveness in the face of stressful, anger-eliciting events. Anxiety, Stress, & Coping. 2021;**34**(4):437-449. DOI: 10.1080/10615806.2021.1918682

[84] Glover N, Miller JD, Lynam DR, Crego C, Widiger TA. The five-factor narcissism inventory: A five-factor measure of narcissistic personality traits. Journal of Personality Assessment. 2012;**94**(5):500-512. DOI: 10.1080/00223891.2012.670680

[85] Boddy CR. Corporate psychopaths, bullying and unfair supervision in the workplace. Journal of Business Ethics. 2011;**100**(3):367-379. DOI: 10.1007/s10551-010-0689-5

[86] Regnaud DA. The Relationship between Top Leaders' Observed Narcissistic Behaviors and Workplace Bullying (Unpublished Dissertation). Minneapolis, MN: Walden University; 2014

[87] Thibault T, Kelloway EK. The dark tetrad at work. Human Performance. 2020;**33**(5):406-424. DOI: 10.1080/08959285.2020.1802728

[88] Bowie V. Workplace violence: A second look. In: Paper Presented to the Crime Prevention Conference. Sydney: University of Western Sydney; 2002. Retrieved from: http://aic.gov.au/media_library/conferences/crimpre/bowie.pdf

[89] Fernández-del-Río E, Ramos-Villagrasa PJ, Barrada JR. Bad guys perform better? The incremental predictive validity of the dark tetrad over big five and honesty-humility. Personality and Individual Differences. 2020;**154**:109700. DOI: 10.1016/j.paid.2019.109700

[90] Pilch I, Turska E. Relationships between Machiavellianism, organizational culture, and workplace bullying: Emotional abuse from the target's and the perpetrator's perspective. Journal of Business Ethics. 2015;**128**(1):83-93. DOI: 10.1007/s10551-014-2081-3

[91] Fernández-del-Río E, Ramos-Villagrasa PJ, Escartín J. The incremental effect of dark personality over the big five in workplace bullying: Evidence from perpetrators and targets. Personality and Individual Differences. 2021;**168**:110291. DOI: 10.1016/j.paid.2020.110291

[92] Meier LL, Semmer NK. Lack of reciprocity, narcissism, anger, and instigated workplace incivility: A moderated mediation model. European Journal of Work and Organizational Psychology. 2013;**22**(4):461-475. DOI: 10.1080/1359432x.2012.654605

[93] Leiter MP, Laschinger HKS, Day A, Oore DG. The impact of civility

interventions on employee social behavior, distress, and attitudes. Journal of Applied Psychology. 2011;**96**(6):1258-1274. DOI: 10.1037/a0024442

[94] Gebben AN, Rivera M, Baz G, Ciarlante K, Min H. Identifying dark personality profiles in working adults. Personality and Individual Differences. 2021;**173**:110630. DOI: 10.1016/j.paid.2021.110630

[95] Cropley DH, Kaufman JC, Cropley AJ. Malevolent creativity: A functional model of creativity in terrorism and crime. Creativity Research Journal. 2008;**20**(2):105-115. DOI: 10.1080/10400410802059424

[96] Dow GT. The Dark Tetrad and malevolent creativity. In: Kapoor H, Kaufman JC, editors. Creativity and Morality. Academic Press; 2023:69-80

[97] Kapoor H, Kaufman JC. Unbound: The relationship among creativity, moral foundations, and dark personality. The Journal of Creative Behavior. 2021;**56**(2):182-193. DOI: 10.1002/jocb.523

[98] Smith MB, Hill AD, Wallace JC, Recendes T, Judge TA. Upsides to dark and downsides to bright personality: A multidomain review and future research agenda. Journal of Management. 2017;**44**(1):191-217. DOI: 10.1177/0149206317733511

[99] Lee SA, Dow GT. Malevolent creativity: Does personality influence malicious divergent thinking? Creativity Research Journal. 2011;**23**(2):73-82

[100] Kapoor H, Khan A. Creativity in context: Presses and task effects in negative creativity. Psychology of Aesthetics, Creativity, and the Arts. 2019;**13**(3):314-321. DOI: 10.1037/aca0000183

[101] Michels M, Molz G, Bermpohl MG, F. The ability to lie and its relations to the dark triad and general intelligence. Personality and Individual Differences. 2020;**166**:110195. DOI: 10.1016/j.paid.2020.110195

[102] Wright GRT, Berry CJ, Catmur C, Bird G. Good liars are neither 'dark' nor self-deceptive. PLoS One. 2015;**10**(6):e0127315. DOI: 10.1371/journal.pone.0127315

[103] Batey M, Hughes D, Mosley A, Owens C, Furnham A. Psychopathy and openness-to-experience as predictors of malevolent and benevolent creativity. Personality and Individual Differences. 2022;**196**:111715. DOI: 10.1016/j.paid.2022.111715

[104] Galang AJR, Castelo VLC, Santos LC, Perlas CMC, Angeles MaB. Investigating the prosocial psychopath model of the creative personality: Evidence from traits and psychophysiology. Personality and Individual Differences. 2016;**100**:28-36. DOI: 10.1016/j.paid.2016.03.081

[105] Kapoor H. The creative side of the dark triad. Creativity Research Journal. 2015;**27**(1):58-67. DOI: 10.1080/10400419.2014.961775

[106] Lebuda I, Figura B, Karwowski M. Creativity and the dark triad: A meta-analysis. Journal of Research in Personality. 2021;**92**:104088. DOI: 10.1016/j.jrp.2021.104088

[107] Jia X, Wang Q, Lin L. The relationship between childhood neglect and malevolent creativity: The mediating effect of the dark triad personality. Frontiers in Psychology. 2020;**11**:613695. DOI: 10.3389/fpsyg.2020.613695

[108] Modic D, Palomäki J, Drosinou M, Laakasuo M. The dark triad and

willingness to commit insurance fraud. Cogent Psychology. 2018;**5**(1):1469579. DOI: 10.1080/23311908.2018.1469579

[109] Kircaburun K, Jonason PK, Griffiths MD. The dark tetrad traits and problematic social media use: The mediating role of cyberbullying and cyberstalking. Personality and Individual Differences. 2018;**135**:264-269. DOI: 10.1016/j.paid.2018.07.034

[110] Nurse JRC. Cybercrime and you: How criminals attack and the human factors that they seek to exploit. In: Attrill-Smith A, Fullwood C, Keep M, Kuss DJ, editors. The Oxford Handbook of Cyberpsychology. New York, NY: Oxford University Press; 2019. pp. 663-690

[111] American Psychiatric Association. Diagnostic and Statistical Manual of Mental Disorders. 5th ed., Text Revision. Washington, DC: APA; 2013

[112] Colman AM. A Dictionary of Psychology. Oxford, England: Oxford Quick Reference; 2015

[113] Mathieu C, Babiak P. Corporate psychopathy and abusive supervision: Their influence on employees' job satisfaction and turnover intentions. Personality and Individual Differences. 2016;**91**:102-106

[114] Miller EK, Cohen JD. An integrative theory of prefrontal cortex function. Annual Review of Neuroscience. 2001;**24**(1):167-202

[115] Bereby-Meyer Y, Shalvi S. Deliberate honesty. Current Opinion in Psychology. 2015;**6**:195-198

[116] Vazsonyi AT, Mikuška J, Kelley EL. It's time: A meta-analysis on the self control-deviance link. Journal of Criminal Justice. 2017;**48**:48-63

[117] Knoch D, Pascual-Leone A, Meyer K, Treyer V, Fehr E. Diminishing reciprocal fairness by disrupting the right prefrontal cortex. Science. 2006;**314**(5800):829-832

[118] Abe N, Greene JD, Kiehl KA. Reduced engagement of the anterior cingulate cortex in the dishonest decision-making of incarcerated psychopaths. Social Cognitive and Affective Neuroscience. 2018;**13**(8):797-807

[119] Zhu L, Jenkins AC, Set E, Scabini D, Knight RT, Chiu PH, et al. Damage to dorsolateral prefrontal cortex affects tradeoffs between honesty and self interest. Nature Neuroscience. 2014;**17**(10):1319-1321

[120] Tost H, Champagne FA, Meyer-Lindenberg A. Environmental influence in the brain, human welfare and mental health. Nature Neuroscience. 2015;**18**(10):1421-1431

[121] Speer SP, Smidts A, Boksem MA. Cognitive control and dishonesty. Trends in Cognitive Sciences. 2022;**26**(9):796-808

[122] Barnes CM, Schaubroeck J, Huth M, Ghumman S. Lack of sleep and unethical conduct. Organizational Behavior and Human Decision Processes. 2011;**115**(2):169-180

[123] Shalvi S, Eldar O, Bereby-Meyer Y. Honesty requires time (and lack of justifications). Psychological Science. 2012;**23**(10):1264-1270

[124] Zhang H, Shi Y, Zhou ZE, Ma H, Tang H. Good people do bad things: How anxiety promotes unethical behavior through intuitive and automatic processing. Current Psychology. 2020;**39**:720-728

[125] Tepper BJ. Consequences of abusive supervision. Academy of Management Journal. 2000;**43**(2):178-190

[126] Mikołajewska E, Prokopowicz P, Chow Y, Masiak J, Mikołajewski D, Wójcik GM, et al. From neuroimaging to computational modeling of burnout: The traditional versus the fuzzy approach—A review. Applied Sciences. 2022;**12**(22):11524

[127] Boddy CR. Organisational psychopaths: A ten year update. Management Decision. 2015

[128] Boddy CR. Corporate psychopaths and organizational type. Journal of Public Affairs. 2010;**10**(4):300-312

[129] Čopková R, Araňošová A. The relationship of dark triad and job satisfaction among helping professionals. Individual & Society. 2020;**23**(3):18-33

[130] Eisenbarth H, Hart CM, Sedikides C. Do psychopathic traits predict professional success? Journal of Economic Psychology. 2018;**64**:130-139

[131] Higgs M. The good, the bad and the ugly: Leadership and narcissism. Journal of change management. 2009;**9**(2):165-178

[132] Galvin BM, Lange D, Ashforth BE. Narcissistic organizational identification: Seeing oneself as central to the organization's identity. Academy of Management Review. 2015;**40**(2):163-181

[133] Nai A, Maier J. Is negative campaigning a matter of taste? Political attacks, incivility, and the moderating role of individual differences. American Politics Research. 2021 May;**49**(3):269-281

[134] Templer KJ. Dark personality, job performance ratings, and the role of political skill: An indication of why toxic people may get ahead at work. Personality and Individual Differences. 2018;**124**:209-214

[135] Lainidi O, Karakasidou E, Montgomery A. Dark triad, impulsiveness and honesty-humility in the prisoner's dilemma game: The moderating role of gender. Merits. 2022;**2**(4):387-399

[136] Al-Shatti E, Ohana M. Impression management and career related outcomes: A systematic literature review. Frontiers in Psychology. 2021;**12**:701694

[137] Torres-Marín J, Navarro-Carrillo G, Carretero-Dios H. Differentiating the traits of the dark tetrad in their linkages with humor styles, dispositions toward ridicule and laughter, and comic styles. Personality and Individual Differences. 2022;**185**:111281. DOI: 10.1016/j.paid.2021.111281

[138] Martin RA, Lastuk JM, Jeffery J, Vernon PA, Veselka L. Relationships between the dark triad and humor styles: A replication and extension. Personality and Individual Differences. 2012;**52**(2):178-182. DOI: 10.1016/j.paid.2011.10.010

[139] Bereczkei T. Machiavellian intelligence hypothesis revisited: What evolved cognitive and social skills may underlie human manipulation. Evolutionary Behavioral Sciences. 2018;**12**(1):32-51. DOI: 10.1037/ebs0000096

[140] Baloch MA, Meng F, Xu Z, Cepeda-Carrion I, Danish, Bari MW. Dark triad, perceptions of organizational politics and counterproductive work behaviors: The moderating effect of political skills. Frontiers in Psychology. 2017;**8**:1972. DOI: 10.3389/fpsyg.2017.01972

[141] Belschak FD, Den Hartog DN, De Hoogh AHB. Angels and demons: The effect of ethical leadership on Machiavellian employees' work behaviors.

Frontiers in Psychology. 2018;**9**:1082. DOI: 10.3389/fpsyg.2018.01082

[142] Palmer JC, Komarraju M, Carter MZ, Karau SJ. Angel on one shoulder: Can perceived organizational support moderate the relationship between the dark triad traits and counterproductive work behavior? Personality and Individual Differences. 2017;**110**:31-37. DOI: 10.1016/j.paid.2017.01.018

[143] Choi Y. A study of the effect of perceived organizational support on the relationship between narcissism and job-related attitudes of Korean employees. Cogent Business & Management. 2019;**6**(1):1573486. DOI: 10.1080/23311975.2019.1573486

[144] Spurk D, Keller AC, Hirschi A. Do bad guys get ahead or fall behind? Relationships of the dark triad of personality with objective and subjective career success. Social Psychological and Personality Science. 2016;**7**(2):113-121

[145] Rasool SF, Wang M, Tang M, Saeed A, Iqbal J. How toxic workplace environment effects the employee engagement: The mediating role of organizational support and employee wellbeing. International Journal of Environmental Research and Public Health. 2021;**18**(5):2294

[146] Austin PE. Baring Brothers and the Birth of Modern Finance. England, UK: Routledge; 2015

[147] Volmer J, Koch IK, Göritz AS. The bright and dark sides of leaders' dark triad traits: Effects on subordinates' career success and well-being. Personality and Individual Differences. 2016;**101**:413-418. DOI: 10.1016/j.paid.2016.06.046

[148] Babiak P, Hare RD. Snakes In Suits: When Psychopaths Go to Work. Los Angeles, California, United States of America: Regan Books/Harper Collins Publishers; 2006

Chapter 4

Counterproductive Workplace Behaviors (CWBs): Antecedents and Outcomes

Ugwu Callistus Chinwuba

Abstract

In the recent decades, counterproductive workplace behaviors (CWBs), a willful and intentional acts by members of organizations that harm organizations and their stakeholders have attracted the interest of organizational researchers due to its prevalence and huge negative impacts on organizations and their members. Globally, businesses have suffered immerse financial losses as well as damage to human capital development leading to feelings of dissatisfaction and distress culminating in intention to quit the organization as a result of CWBs. The present study therefore focused on exploring a number of theoretical and empirical organizational and individual antecedents of CWBs. As there are still lack of adequate understanding of the behavior especially as it concerns the predictors, further studies are necessary to gain more insight about the behavior that will enable stakeholders understand the motivational roots of the behavior which will aid in designing appropriate remedy on how to curb and mitigate the behaviors.

Keywords: counterproductive work behaviors, antecedents, outcomes, organizations, stakeholders

1. Introduction

Counterproductive workplace behaviors (CWBs) have attracted much research attention in the recent times due to its prevalence and negative outcomes to organizations and its members. Zhao et al. [1] assert that "of all the negative behaviors that employees develop at work, none are more prevalent than CWBs" (p. 219). The behaviors which are intentional acts by members of organizations run counter to the legitimate interest of organizations and pose harmful and detrimental effect to organizational well-being. As forms of deviant behaviors, CWBs are voluntary and intentional acts by members of organization that violates significant organizational norms and threaten the well-being of organizations, its members or both. In fact, CWBs are deliberate acts that harm the organization or its members [2]. According to Spector and Fox [3], the behaviors are defined as "volitional acts that harm organizations and their stakeholders (e.g., clients, coworkers, customers, and supervisors." (p.151). CWBs are peculiar and differ from other common negative acts since they are not accidental but are intended specifically to damage organization's reputation. The behaviors come in forms of fraud, theft, sabotage, cyber-loafing, vandalism, pilfering, absence and lateness to work, long break, harassment, gossiping, drug use, sloppy work, intentional slow, etc. [4, 5]. Indeed, behaviors such as these are dysfunctional to organizations because they violate important organizational norms and harm organizational well-being.

Literature distinguishes two kinds of CWBs – (i) CWBs directed towards organization (CBWs-O) and (ii) CWBs directed towards people in the organizations (CWBs-P) [6]. CWBs-O are behaviors directed towards organizations such as sabotage, theft and fraud, or lateness to work, leaving early from work, taking excessive breaks, deliberately working slowly, wasting resources, etc. On the other hand, CWBs-P are acts mainly directed towards people working in the organization which come in form sexual harassment, verbal abuse, stealing among coworkers, choosing favorites, gossiping among colleagues, etc. Even though these two kinds of behavior bear significant relationships [7], they differ in their relationship with variables such as citizenship behaviors, perceived justices, situational constraints, personal traits, etc. [8, 9]. Collectively, CWBs are deviant behavior that violate significant organizational norms, reduces the efficiency and job performances of its members and basically threatens the health and well-being of organizations and its members.

Empirical evidence shows that CWBs are one of the most serious problems organizations are facing in many countries [10]. Studies have shown that CWBs result in severe economic and social threats to organizations. For instance, Dineen et al. [11] report that in the US, the cost of fraud and theft alone to organizations is estimated at over $50 billion annually; and the overall losses caused by other forms of CWBs are quite huge. Earlier, Murphy [12] reported that employee deviance and delinquency have accounted for between $6 billion and $200 billion of organizational loss annually. Expectedly, Harper [13] found that a good number of employees (33–75%) have at one time or the other shown to have engaged in one form of CWB or the other in serving an organization. Globally, businesses have suffered losses of about US$2.9 trillion annually due to fraudulent activities [14, 15]. Ugwu and Ogbogu [16] assert that in developing countries such as Nigeria where data may not exist, the cost arising from deviant workplace behaviors may be quite huge and bewildering. Apart from financial loses to organizations, engagement in CWB also affects the human capital of the organization, as it has been suggested that the behavior could lead to feelings of dissatisfaction and distress, culminating in intention to quit the organization [17, 18]. Thus, CWBs not only cost organizations fortunes but also affect the productivity as well as create discomfort to members of organization, compromise the quality of organizational life, damage property and at the same time hurt organizational reputation as a whole [19].

The focus of the present study is therefore on the antecedents and outcomes of CWBs. This is necessitated by the increase of deviant behaviors in organizations which raises the questions about ethics and moral issues in workplaces. Therefore, there is the need to gain insight into the likely causes by the managers of organizations in order to curb them. Even though several decades of study have been devoted to identifying varieties of individual and situational antecedents of CWBs, some authors such as Cohen [20] observe that there is still lack of adequate understanding of the behavior especially as it concerns the predictors. Further studies on the antecedents and outcomes of CWBs are therefore necessary so as to shade more light which will enable stakeholders understand the motivational roots of the behavior in order to design approaches to curb and mitigate the behaviors.

1.1 Antecedents of CWBs

Given the prevalence and the accompanying negative effects of CWBs, it is important to isolate the antecedents of the behavior. The antecedents can be explored from the perspectives of individual (personality or cognitive traits) and situational (job/organizational) variables. In order to have a better understanding of the behavior, the theoretical and empirical perspectives is examined.

2. Theoretical perspectives

2.1 Social exchange theory (SET)

The framework of social exchange theory (SET) can be used in understanding CWBs. The theory developed by Blau [21] posits that human relationships are based on subjective cost–benefit analysis. More importantly, the theory assumes that social relationships are based on trust that acts of goodwill will be reciprocated. The SET has been used to understand workplace behaviors such as CWBs, perception of justices, etc. For instance, in a meta-analytic study, Colquitt et al. [22] employed SET as a dominant approach to determine reactions to justice perceptions and found strong relationships between the dimensions of justice and indicators of social exchange. Specifically, factors of social exchange such as trust, commitment, organizational support, leader-member exchange were found to be significantly related to justice perception, task performance and citizenship behavior [22].

One of the instances of implementing SET in organizational research is in the explanation of organizational loyalty (e.g. [23]). According to Eisenberger et al. [23], employees have a general idea about the extent to which organizations value their contributions and cares about them in terms of organizational support. Accordingly, when employees perceive that organization values their contribution, cares and supports them, they become satisfied and reciprocate by maintaining high level of performance and commitment to the organization. In other words, employees become obligated to maintain high level of performance and commitment under high levels of perceived organizational support. Conversely, employees who perceive that their organization does not provide the needed support and care would be dissatisfied with their jobs and reciprocate by engaging in some form of retaliatory behaviors like CWBs. Indeed, the social exchange theory and norm of reciprocity suggest that when employees are dissatisfied with their organizations, their boss or coworkers, they may reciprocate with deviant work behaviors such as withholding effort, arriving late, taking long break times, leaving early, or engaging in CWBs directed to colleagues such as incivility, playing mean pranks, or even sabotaging their efforts, etc. In a meta-analytic study of factors associated with workplace aggression, Hershcovis et al. [9] found that job dissatisfaction is related to CWBs in form of organizational aggression. Judge et al. [24] as well as Dalal [25] reported a negative relationship between job satisfaction and some measures of deviant workplace behaviors. Judge et al. [7] established that employees engaged more in CWBs on days when they were less satisfied with their jobs than the days they were more satisfied. According to Bies and Tripp [26], employees' workplace aggression reflects an attempt to restore justice to an unfair organizational situation. Also, previous studies found that indicators of workplace social exchange – leader-member exchange and perceived organizational support – may be associated with perception of justices and workplace attitudes and behaviors [27, 28], and that violation of psychological contract is associated with employees' performance and absenteeism [29].

2.2 Stress-emotion theory

The Stress-Emotion theory developed by Spector and Fox [3] focuses on both situational and personal factors of CWBs. The situational factors considered are job stressors which refer to any frustrating condition in organizational life that hinder the performance of work or job activities. Job stressors may include organizational constraints, unmanaged conflicts, work overload, role conflict and ambiguity, lack of autonomy and support, etc. According to the model any frustrating condition in organizational life that interferes with the goals and job performance increases the chances of CWBs in employees. The model further argues that when such frustrating condition occurs, individuals may experience negative emotions which in turn may compel people to engage in aggressive behavior as a strategy to reduce the emotionally unpleasant condition [30, 31]. Thus, the model describes the processes that create forms of aggression that are typically impulsive and with the intent to cause harm and release frustration.

Literature distinguishes between impulsive (reactive) aggression and instrumental (proactive) aggression. Impulsive aggression is based on negative affect that may lead to offensive reactions beyond one's control while instrumental aggression has to do with aggression that is intentionally carried out in line with one's personal goals [32]. Thus, CWBs may have the attributes of both impulsive and instrumental aggression. For instance, employees who engage in CWBs may be as a result of impulsive anger arising from organizational stressors as well as with the intent to hurt a colleague so as to have advantage in the hierarchy of the work. Therefore, the stress-emotional model is a combination of both cognitive processes that could capture the intentional and, sometimes instrumental nature of CWBs. The theory therefore integrates two important traditions of research on aggressive behavior, i.e., the frustration-aggression hypothesis which focuses on effects that negative emotions and affect regulation can exert on aggression; and the social cognitive processes which addresses the processes that promote or justify aggression.

The frustration-aggression model holds that in the workplace, certain undesirable events (e.g., constraints) interfere with employees' goal attainment and therefore lead to frustration. When employees are frustrated, they try to overcome their negative feelings by committing some form of aggression, which may be directed towards people or the organization. When the frustration is caused by some organizational factors, people are likely to direct their CWB towards the organization.

Empirical evidences show that high level of negative emotions experienced in the workplace including low emotional stability, low self-control, personality traits, and low job satisfaction increases the likelihood of engaging in CWBs (e.g., [33–35]). Also, Fida et al. [36] found that negative emotions and moral disengagement are strong predictors of CWBs. The stress-emotion model therefore suggests that negative emotions are critical factors in CWBs.

3. Empirical review

In the present study, empirical review of literature examines both organizational and individual factors and their relationships with CWBs.

3.1 Organizational factors

3.1.1 Organizational justice and CWBs

Organizational justice is the extent to which organizations furnish its employees with the right, fair and respectful treatment, adequate and accurate information, resources and rewards. Employees' perception of organizational justice is formed by the overall impressions formed from occasional organizational occurrences and personal appraisals of organizations such as leaders and coworkers [37]. The perceptions tend to influence employees attitudes and behaviors which in turn impact performances and organizational well-being.

Organizational justice is structured along four dimensions: (i) distributive justice, i.e., fairness in allocation of resources and products; (ii) procedural justice, i.e., fairness in ways and procedures decisions are reached vis-à-vis the distribution of resources; (iii) interactional justice, i.e., fairness in interpersonal relations, respectful and adequate treatment; and accessibility of equal opportunities, and (iv) informational justice, i.e., fairness in ways adequate and timely information about the allocation of organizational resources are provided [22, 38].

Empirical studies show that there is a direct negative effect of organizational justice on CWB (e.g., [22, 39]). This suggests that if employees believe that the organization is fair in decision-making, they are more likely to exhibit positive attitudes and behaviors towards the organization, their managers, and their work. On the other hand, decisions seen as unfair may lead employees to cause what they perceive as equivalent damage to restore justice. Social exchange theory and the norm of reciprocity provide the theoretical support for this reasoning, as they suggest that "negative reciprocation serves as a means to restore the balance and eliminates anger and frustration engendered by unfair treatment" ([39], p. 1690). Also, the previous works of Aquino et al. [40] and Ambrose et al. [41] are in support of negative relationship between organizational justice perceptions and CWBs. Thus, perception of injustice seems to be the primary contributory factor of workplace deviance. The idea that individuals retaliate in response to perceived injustice is based on the principle of retributive justice. Conversely, perception of fair organizational justice tends to lead to positive outcomes in organizations such as citizenship behavior, high level of job motivation and satisfaction, trust, commitment, and productivity, loyalty [42, 43].

3.1.2 Organizational climate and CWBs

Organizational climate refers to the prevailing social climate or atmosphere in work settings concerning polices, practices and procedures in organizations (e.g., [44]). According to Ivancevitch et al. ([45], p. 10), "organizational climate is a set of work characteristics perceived directly or indirectly by the employees that is assumed to be a major force in influencing employee behavior". As part of psychological process, perceptions of organizational climate enables employees recognize what behaviors are expected and rewarded. The perceptions therefore reflect employees' impressions of work environment which influence their levels of stress, job satisfaction, commitment and performance which in turn have implications for overall organizational productivity [44].

Organizational ethical climate remains one specific perception when it comes to perception of organizational climate. Organizational ethical climate involves contextual factors showing employees' knowledge of moral obligation, their beliefs of what ethically correct behavior is and how the organization's ethical issues are handled by the organization. Literature suggests five types of ethical climate including instrumental, caring, independence, rules, law and code (e.g., [46]). While instrumental ethical climate is considered as a negative type of climate because of its self-serving function, the other four types are considered as positive as they tend to foster the emergence of positive organizational attitude because of their concern for the well-being of others, for laws or organizational policies and procedures to be followed and adherence to one's personal and ethical beliefs [46, 47].

Ethical work climate therefore furnishes employees with the information regarding appropriate behavior in a work environment. As such negative perception of overall organizational climate and ethical climate may tend to have immediate implications for CWBs as such perception reflects employees' impression that the prevailing work environment of the organization is unpleasant and dissatisfactory. In relation with SET, if employees perceive that organization is not meeting up with its own part of obligation in terms of providing the needed work environment that foster satisfaction, they are likely to reciprocate by engaging in some forms of deviant behavior as against those who perceive a supportive organizational climate. Therefore, if ethical climate promotes ethical work behavior, employees are less likely to engage in unethical behavior (e.g. [48]). Empirical evidence has shown support that ethical work climate is negatively associated with unethical organizational behavior. For instance, Martin and Cullen's [46] meta-analytic study indicated that positive ethical work climates were negatively associated with dysfunctional organizational behaviors. Specifically, the studies found that ethical work climate was negatively related to CWBs and that deviance in organization attenuated in an ethical caring climate [48, 49]. Similarly, Chernyak-Hai and Tziner [50] found that the employees' perceptions of overall organizational climate as well as ethical climate were negatively related to CWBs, i.e., the better perceived overall organizational climate and ethical climate, the lower the reported CWBs. In general, work environment or climate perception by the employees adds significant values to individuals and organizations as favorable climate tends to inhibit CWBs while unfavorable one tends to foster deviant workplace behaviors.

3.1.3 Organizational culture and CWBs

Organizational culture refers to shared values, beliefs, and norms that influence the ways employees think, feel, and behave in the workplace [51]. According to Schein [51], organizational culture provides the needed avenue that integrates shared values and beliefs which assist organizations to solve problems and challenges. Therefore, the prevailing organizational culture in the workplace is capable of promoting or hindering CWBs. Griffin and O'Leary-Kelly [52] argue that organizational culture can affect employee behavior positively or negatively. For instance, if the organizational culture disapproves of deviant behaviors and metes out severe sanctions and punishment against it, deviant behaviors can be inhibited but if the culture encourages deviant behavior by building and supporting dysfunctional culture, then deviance will tend to be fostered. According to Griffin and O'Leary [52], dysfunctional culture restrains or confines individuals and group-level abilities which reward mediocre individual and group-level performance and is likely to foster rancorous cycle of workplace deviance.

Scholars have argued that favorable organizational culture is linked to positive behaviors such as novel pioneering behavior and citizenship behaviors (e.g. [53, 54]).

A functional organizational culture tends to discourage unhealthy attitudes and behaviors such as absenteeism, deferment, putting little effort into work, taking excessive break, wasting/damaging company property, work incivility, etc. [55]. When the culture of organization is perceived as favorable, there is tendency for CWBs to decline [54]. Kidwell and Valentine further argue that when the prevailing culture is organizationally induced and rewarding, employees tend to exhibit more positive behaviors and by implication less likely to engage in CWBs. Adenike [56] argue that organizational climate or culture influences employees' motivation, behaviors, attitudes and potentials which in turn promotes productivity and effectiveness. In contrast, poor work environment tend to encourage deviant behaviors such as cyber-loafing, malingering, rescheduling assignment, putting little effort to work, taking excessive breaks, wasting/damaging company resources, work inactivity, etc. [55]. In general, the culture of organizations and how it is inculcated and perceived by employees and by extension how well employees are treated determine the effectiveness of organization.

3.1.4 Organizational politics and CWBs

Politics is ubiquitous and has become a way of life in many organizations. Perceptions of organizational politics have received increasing attention in management literature and have emerged as a good predictor of job outcomes and job performance (e.g. [57]). Mintzberg [58] defined organizational politics as "individual or group behavior that is informal, ostensibly parochial, typically divisive, and above all, in a technical sense, illegitimate – sanctioned neither by formal authority, accepted ideology, nor certified expertise (although it may exploit any one of these)" (p. 172). According to Kacmar and Baron [59], "organizational politics are actions perceived by individuals as directed toward the goal of furthering their own self-interests without regard for the well-being of others or their organizations" (p. 4). Similarly, Witt et al. [60] stated that "organizational politics is a phenomenon in which members of the organization attempt directly or indirectly, in order to manipulate the behavior of other members by means of disapproved prescribed standard operating procedures or informal standards mostly in attempt to achieve objectives of individuals or groups" (p. 12). Ferris et al. ([61], p. 25) listed examples of political behaviors to include but not limited to "coalition building, favoritism-based pay and promotion decision, and backstabbing with the intention to benefit, protect, or enhance self-interests, often without regard for the well-being of their organization or colleagues". In addition, Andrews and Kacmar [62] included bypassing the chain of command to gain approval, going through unapproved channels to obtain special favor, and lobbying high level managers just prior to promotion decisions. Other forms of political behavior may include withholding information from colleagues, failing to enforce policies and procedures appropriately, using flattery to gain favor, shifting blame, and maligning others to make oneself relevance.

There are three dimensions of behaviors characterizing organizational politics identified by literature including – (i) General Political Behavior (GPB), which describe the behavior of individuals who behave in a self-serving manner to achieve desired outcomes; (ii) Go Along to Get Ahead (GAGA), which consists of lack of action by individuals (e.g., remain silent) in order to secure valued outcomes; and (iii) Pay and Promotion Policies (PPP), which involves organizations behaving politically through the policies it enacts [63]. Thus, researchers of organizational politics have focused on perceptions of such behavior which is subjective and as a state of mind may differ from person to person. Therefore, perceptions of organizational politics "involve an individual's attribution to behaviors of self-serving intent, defined as an individual's subjective evaluation about the extent to which the work environment is characterized by co-workers and supervisors who demonstrates such self-serving behaviors" ([64], p. 90).

Power, influence, and politics are likely to have obvious negative effects on organizations and its members. Empirical evidences have established that perception of organizational politics impact negatively on both workers and the work they perform (e.g., [59, 65]). For instance, studies have suggested that perception of organizational politics is negatively related to undesirable job performance outcomes including poor communication among employees, diminished job attitudes, employee turnover, job dissatisfaction, job stress and strain, job burnout, CWBs (e.g., [66, 67]). From the perspective of SET and norm of reciprocity as well as that of stress-emotion model, employees are likely be motivated to engage in CWBs in response to perceived organizational stressors such as injustice, psychological contract breaches, and other organizational constraints that interfere with the achievement of personal goals at work [68, 69]. When work environment is characterized by power play it is considered stressful; and when confronted with such organizational stressors, employees are likely to retaliate by engaging in CWBs in order to restore their sense of equity and justice [70, 71]. Indeed, studies have shown that organizational politics is positively associated with organizational stressors such as perceived organizational injustice, psychological contract breach and other constraints that hinder employees from job performance and achievement of their personal goals [72, 73]. In fact, more recent studies have shown that perceived organizational politics is positively related to CWBs (e.g., [74, 75]). Also, Meisler et al. [76] found a positive relationship between perceived organizational politics and CWBs. Thus, organizational politics is considered another organizational variable that is stressful which in turn may compel some organizational members to engage in workplace deviant behavior in order to maintain a sense of balance and equity.

4. Leader-member exchange (LMX) and CWBs

Leader-member exchange (LMX), an aspect of employees' workplace perception regarding organizational issues can impact CWBs. The exchange relates to quality of relationship between leaders and his followers. The core tenet of LMX is that leaders treat followers differently in a series of work-related exchange, and based on the relationships, leaders consider followers as either trusted or untrusted thereby exhibiting differential treatment towards each group. Trusted (in-group) followers are treated with high quality relationship while untrusted (out-group) members are treated with low quality exchange. Thus, LMX attempts to understand how quality of the relationships develops as well as the impacts the relationships has on relevant organizational activities and processes. According to Bauer and Green [77], "high quality LMX indicates high level of information exchange, interaction, trust, respect, support, mutual influence, and reward, while low quality LMX points to low level of interaction, trust, formal relations, one-directional influence, (manager-employee), limited support, and few rewards" (p. 36). Expectedly, differential treatment can be problematic for lower quality relationship individuals as they are more likely to view differential treatment as being unfair. Therefore, leaders' differential treatments can lead to perception of inequity with lower quality exchange individuals being more likely to engage in deviant work behaviors than high quality exchange persons. This is consistent with the tenets of SET and the norm of reciprocity which suggests that individuals engage in relationships on the basis of cost–benefit analysis and tend to respond to each other with in a commensurate behavior [21, 78].

Furthermore, in line with Kelloway et al. [79] suggestion that passive leadership behavior can foster increased level of stress; expectedly low LMX constitutes environmental stressors as their subordinates are likely to receive less supervisory attention, support, consideration and communication leading to the possibility of engaging in CWBs. Indeed, studies are replete with issues, concerns, and impact LMX has on organizational outcomes and behaviors of followers (e.g., [80, 81]). For instance, LMX is reported to affect employees' motivation in several areas of organizational functioning, increasing or decreasing opportunities, sense of empowerment, emotional support, and cooperative interactions, including loyalty, respect and obligation (e.g., [82, 83]). Also, previous studies have actually shown that high levels of LMX correlates positively with citizenship behaviors (e.g. [42, 84]). Concerning deviant behavior, de Oliveira et al. [85] reported a direct negative relationship between LMX and CWBs. Also, Newton and Perlow [86] found that LMX relations correlated negatively with CWBs such that individuals with low quality leader-member relations exhibited CWBs than subordinates with higher quality leader-member relations. Thus, high-quality relationships have been found to be positively related to performance, retention, job satisfaction, organizational commitment, and organizational citizenship behaviors [80]. In contrast, research shows that low-quality relationships, low leadership consideration, and abusive supervision tend to lead to deviant workplace behaviors [87].

5. Individual variables

5.1 Personality and CWBs

Personality traits can be defined as a relatively enduring configuration of thoughts, feelings, and behaviors that cause the individual to respond in specific ways to particular circumstances [88]. It is important to identify personality characteristics that may relate to CWBs since the behavior is an act based on individual choice [34]. The personality factors of interest in the present study include the Big Five Personality Trait, Dark Triads and personal values.

5.2 Big five personality factors

The Five-Factor Model (FFM or Big Five) which comprises agreeableness, conscientiousness, extraversion, neuroticism, and openness to experience has been globally accepted as a valid structure of personality traits and widely employed by organizational researchers [89, 90]. Agreeableness is related to cooperativeness, good-nature, considerate and kindness of persons; conscientiousness describes one who is careful, industrious, hardworking, achievement oriented, persistent, dependable, and orderliness; extraversion refers to one who has preference for social interactions and need for stimulation; neuroticism refers to individuals who are anxious, hostile, and a general inability to deal with negative emotions; while openness to experience refers to exploratory behaviors, active imagination, autonomy, and nonconformity [34, 89].

Regarding the impact of personality traits on CWBs, Salgado [89] in a meta-analysis found that agreeableness and conscientiousness were valid predictors of deviant behaviors, while Berry et al. [8] found that among the Big Five, only agreeableness, conscientiousness, and neuroticism were significantly related to CWBs. Spector [90] suggests that personality affects CWBs through cognitive-emotional processes and; in line with the cognitive-motivational-relational theory [91, 92], it could be argued that agreeableness and neuroticism are predictors of CWBs. An employee who is cooperative and kind may be less likely to respond negatively to situations she/he encounters but not so for antagonistic individuals. In contrast, a person who is predominantly anxious and negative towards life in general may tend to experience more negative emotions thereby compelling the individual to be more prone to deviant behaviors. In line with this reasoning, de Oliveira et al. [85] reported that agreeableness was negatively correlated to CWBs while neuroticism was positively correlated to CWBs. Also, Bowling and Eschleman [33] found that agreeableness and conscientiousness was negatively related to both CWBs-O and CWBs-P which also aligns with the findings of Mount et al. [34]. In a similar study, Bolton et al. [93] found that agreeableness and conscientiousness predicted CWBs. Again, Waheeda and Hafidz [94] reported significant negative relationship between agreeableness, conscientiousness and CWBs. Conscientiousness was found to be negatively correlated to seven dimensions of CWBs (theft and related behavior, destruction of property, misuse of information, poor quality work, alcohol use, drug use, inappropriate verbal actions, and inappropriate physical actions) while agreeableness was found to be negatively correlated to only three dimensions of CWBs (theft and related behavior, misuse of information, and poor quality work). Openness was found to be negatively correlated to theft and related behavior, while neuroticism was found to be positively correlated to poor quality work only. Extraversion was not correlated to any of the CWBs dimensions [94]. From the aforementioned studies, it can be seen that personality can be a predictor of CWBs, with agreeableness and conscientiousness being consistent predictors of it.

5.3 Individual values and CWBs

There have been extensive studies on values either in isolation or in combination with other constructs [95, 96]. However, there are paucity of studies with regard to the relationship between values and CWBs. Values can be defined as "principles for action encompassing abstract goals in life and modes of conduct that an individual or a collective considers preferable across contexts and situations" ([97], p. 364). Values can be seen as a guiding principle, representing one's motivational goal in life which makes it worthwhile exploring the relationship with CWBs since the behavior is an act of personal volition. Schwartz [98] proposes ten individual values including achievement, benevolence, conformity, hedonism, power, security, self-direction, stimulation, tradition, and universalism. Achievement is related to personal success, competence according to social standards; benevolence refers to kindness, fairness, forgiving and maintaining good interpersonal relationship; conformity entails restraint of actions, inclinations and impulses likely to upset or harm others and violate social expectations and norms; hedonism relates to pleasure-seeking or sensuous gratification; power refers to control or dominance over people and resources, need for social status and prestige; security implies safety, harmony and stability of society, of relationships and of self; self-direction involves independent thought and action expressed in choosing, creating and exploring; stimulation refers to excitement, arousal, novelty and taking up challenge in life; tradition is respect for social rules and others, acceptance of customs and ideas of one's culture; while universalism refers to understanding, appreciation, tolerance and protection for the well-being of all people and for nature.

Concerning the relationship between individual values and CWBs, Waheeda and Hafidz [94] found that hedonism and power was positively correlated to CWBs; while benevolence and conformity was negatively correlated to CWBs. Security was not related to any dimension of CWBs. Again, conformity, tradition, benevolence, and achievement were negatively correlated to some dimensions of CWBs such as theft and related behaviors, alcohol use, drug use, misuse of time and resources, poor attendance, inappropriate behaviors; while hedonism, self-direction and stimulation was positively correlated to alcohol use and drug use dimensions of CWBs. Tradition was found to be negatively correlated to alcohol use, drug use, and inappropriate verbal actions dimensions of CWBs. Interestingly, universalism was negatively related to three dimensions of CWBs (misuse of time and resources, poor attendance, and poor quality work and drug use [94].

In an earlier study exploring the individual values and overall CWBs, Bruursema [99] found that benevolence was negatively correlated to CWBs while hedonism and stimulation was positively correlated to CWBs. None of the values were significantly correlated to CWBs directed to persons in the organization; but it was found that benevolence, achievement, and stimulation were all correlated to CWBs directed towards the organization. Based on the few available empirical studies, it seems that individual values are good predictors of CWBs; though further studies are needed.

6. Dark triads personality and CWBs

The term Dark Triads was used by Paulhus and Williams [100] to describe three personality traits, i.e. psychopath, Machiavellianism, and narcissism associated with deviant behavior. Psychopath-type personality describes individuals lacking in conscience, empathy, remorsefulness and accountability; and known for impulsiveness; narcissism describes someone who has inflated ego and self-image, full of self-admiration and self-exaggeration; while Machiavellianism describes a person who is morally disengaged, morally depraved and manipulative in nature. Although, the three personality traits are distinct in style, they have the common characteristic of obvious and open exploitation of others.

Lately, the Dark Triads of personality have received research attention and may be considered possible antecedents of CWBs [101]. This is because Barlett [102] found that all the Dark Triad traits are associated with aggression. Geel et al. [103] found that the Dark Triad traits are related to traditional bullying and cyber bullying behavior in adolescents and adults. Based on the perspective of SET, Palmer et al. [104] found that individuals who scored high on the Dark Triad traits are less inclined to engage in CWBs when there is high perception of organizational support. Also, O'Boyle et al. [105] in a meta-analytic study found a weak, moderate, and relatively strong relationship between psychopath, Machiavellianism, narcissism and CWBs respectively. Earlier, Grijalva and Newman [106] found that among the Dark Triads, narcissism alone predicted CWBs. Wu and Lebreton [107] suggest that deviant behavior, the hallmark of Dark Triads of personality may be the outcome of deviant personality and this reasoning may be the justification for the likely association between Dark Triads of personality and CWBs. The lack of empathy, remorse, accountability and impulsivity characteristic of psychopath; the inflated ego, self-admiration and exaggeration characteristics of narcissistic-type personality; and the moral corruption, moral depravity and manipulative tendency characteristics of Machiavellianism may work to engender motivation for counterproductive work behaviors in organizations.

Specifically, Wu and Lebreton [107] assert that psychopathic-type personalities are related to CWBs as those with high level of the traits tend to harm others in pursuit of their personal interest. Consequently, they distract the attention of others from a particular task to pursue their own agenda. Again, their lack of conscience and the desire to achieve their needs at the detriment of others may push them to engage in CWBs [105]. Earlier, Hare and Neuman [108] reported that psychopath-type personalities are more inclined to engage in CWBs. In subsequent studies, Scherer et al. [109] and Smith and Lilienfeld [101] found that psychopath is associated with CWBs. Also, Baloch et al. [110] found that psychopath is positively related to CWBs with organizational politics mediating the relationship between psychopath and CWBs.

With regard to narcissism, Spector [111] argued that inflated self-ego is a trait characteristics of individuals who have high level of narcissism. According to Wu and Lebreton [107], narcissistic-type personality individuals may do whatever that is possible to exaggerate themselves at the detriment of others. The trait of over-inflated self-ego and self-exaggeration, to the extent of discrediting others may increase the chances of narcissistic-personality individuals to engage in CWBs. Expectedly, Penny and Spector [112] as well as Grijalva and Newman [106] found that narcissism is positively associated with CWBs. In a more recent study, Baloch et al. [110] found that narcissism is positively related to CWBs with organizational politics mediating the relationship between narcissism and CWBs.

In the case of Machiavellianism, individuals who have high level of the trait are known for their moral depravity, moral disengagement and manipulative tendencies. According to Wu and Lebreton [107], they are highly inclined to do whatever is possible to achieve their goals. Since they believe that the end justifies the means, it does not matter whatever means they use to achieve their goals provided it is achieved. The ruthless and unethical behaviors of individuals who possess high level of Machiavellian traits are the strong base for the contention that they are more inclined to engage in counterproductive work behaviors. Also, Machiavellian individuals are likely to behave impulsively and in an irresponsible manner when dealing with others. Because of their moral rectitude and manipulative tendencies, they are not concerned and care less about the consequences of their behaviors. The unemotional and callous nature of behaviors of Machiavellian-type personalities are strong indications that such individuals are likely be involved in counterproductive work behaviors. Consequently, Kish-Gephart et al. [113] as well as O'Bolye et al. [105] established that Machiavellianism is positively correlated with CWBs. In addition, Baloch et al. [110] found that Machiavellianism is positively related to CWBs with organizational politics mediating the relationship between Machiavellianism and CWBs.

7. Outcomes of CWBs

There are all manners of CWBs with each impacting organizations differently. For instance, corruption one of the indicators of CWBs has been shown to lower overall morale and doing damage to public trust in the organizations. Also, the issue of data theft, another indices of CWBs could be a major liability for organizations as it could lead to legal tussles and fines as well as causing irrevocable breach of trust between stakeholders and organizations. Time theft arguably has been shown to lead to decreased productivity and profit as well as overall employee morale. Fraud, embezzlement and bribery can have serious consequences for a company's reputation and lose of trust as well as leading to revenue loss. Berry et al. [14] identified hyper-anxiety, job dissatisfaction, and tendency to quit a job as common outcomes of CWBs. CWBs have negative impact on customer evaluation of services, negatively impacting satisfaction and loyalty, and damaging long-term profitability [114, 115]. Thus, CWB leads to unsafe and insecure work environment which may have adverse effects on the performance and well-being of employees and the organization in general. Thus, continuous occurrence of CWBs may create a culture in which the behavior can be easily justified and committed more often by far more individuals leading to long term damage to organizational well-being.

8. Summary and conclusion

CWBs are voluntary acts such as theft, sabotage or doing a work incorrectly that harm organizations. The behaviors are highly prevalent and has negative consequences including huge financial loss and damage to human capital development of organizations. In order for organizations to mitigate incidences of CWBs, gaining insight into the antecedents and outcomes which was the focus of the present work is extremely important. Having identified a number of organizational and individual antecedents of CWBs, it behooves on organizational science researchers and managers to develop policies and programs to reduce incidents of CWBs.

Author details

Ugwu Callistus Chinwuba
Faculty of Management and Social Sciences, Department of Psychology, Madonna University Nigeria, Okija Campus, Anambra State, Nigeria

*Address all correspondence to: callistuschinwuba@gmail.com

References

[1] Zhao H, Peng Z, Sheard G. Workplace ostracism and hospitality employees' CWBs: The joint moderating effects of proactive personality and political skill. International Journal of Hospitality Management. 2013;**33**:219-227

[2] Carpenter NC, Whitman DS, Amrhein R. Uni-level CWBs: A conceptual review and quantitative summary. Journal of Management. 2021;**47**(6):1498-1527

[3] Spector PE, Fox S. A model of counterproductive work behavior. In: Fox S, Spector PE, editors. Counterproductive Workplace Behavior: Investigations of Actors and Targets. Washington, DC: APA; 2005. pp. 151-174

[4] Gruys ML, Sackett PR. Investigating the dimensionality of counterproductive work behavior. International Journal of Selection and Assessment. 2003;**11**:30-42

[5] Spector PE, Fox S, Penney LM, Bruursema K, Goh A, Kessler S. A dimensionality of counter productivity: Are all counterproductive behaviors created equal? Journal of Vocational Behavior. 2006;**68**:446-460

[6] Robinson SL, Benneth RJ. A typology of deviant workplace behavior: A multi-dimensional scale study. Academy of Management Journal. 1995;**38**:555-572

[7] Judge TA, Scott BA, Ilies R. Hostility, job attitudes, and workplace deviance: Test of multi-level model. Journal of Applied Psychology. 2006;**91**:126-138

[8] Berry CM, Ones DS, Sackett PR. Interpersonal deviance, organizational deviance, and their common correlates: A review and meta-analysis. Journal of Applied Psychology. 2007;**92**:410-424

[9] Hershcovis MS, Turner N, Barling J, Arnold KA, Dupre KE, Innes M, et al. Predicting workplace aggression: A meta-analysis. Journal of Applied Psychology. 2007;**92**:228-238

[10] Chappell D, Di Martino V. Violence at Work. 3rd ed. Geneva, Switzerland: International Labor Office; 2006

[11] Dineen BR, Lewicki RJ, Tomlinson EC. Supervisory guidance and behavioral integrity: Relationships with employee citizenship behavior and deviant behavior. Journal of Applied Psychology. 2006;**91**(3):622-635

[12] Murphy KR. Honesty in the Workplace. Belmont, CA: Brooks/Cole; 1993

[13] Harper D. Spotlight abuse-save profits. Industrial Distribution. 1990;**79**:47-51

[14] Berry CM, Carpenter NC, Barratt CL. Do other-reports of counterproductive work behavior provide an incremental contribution over self-report? A meta-analytic comparison. Journal of Applied Psychology. 2012;**97**:613-636

[15] Moore C, Detert JR, Trevino LK, Baker VL, Mayer DM. Why employees do bad things: Moral disengagement and unethical organizational behavior. Personal Psychology. 2012;**65**:1-48

[16] Ugwu CC, Nnamah GN, Ogbogu UC. Job insecurity and deviant workplace behaviors: Buffering role of honesty-humility personality trait. International Journal of Advance Study and Research Work. 2022;**5**(4):1-12

[17] Dunlop PD, Lee K. Workplace deviance, organizational citizenship behavior, and business unit performance: The bad apples do spoil the whole barrel.

Journal of Organizational Behavior. 2004;**25**:67-80

[18] Glomb TM. Workplace anger and aggression: Informing conceptual models with data from specific encounters. Journal of Occupational Health Psychology. 2002;7:20-36

[19] Vardi Y, Weitz E. Misbehavior in Organizations: Theory, Research, and Management. Mahwah, NJ US: Lawrence Erlbaum Associates Publishers; 2004

[20] Cohen A. Are they among us? A conceptual framework of the relationship between the dark triad personality and counterproductive work behaviors (CWBs). Human Resource Management Review. 2016;**26**(1):69-85

[21] Blau P. Exchange and Power in Social Life. New York: Wiley; 1964

[22] Colquitt JA, Scott BA, Rodell JB, Long DM, Zapata CP, Conlon DE, et al. Justice at the millennium, a decade later: A meta-analytic test of social exchange and affect-based perspectives. Journal of Applied Psychology. 2013;**98**(2):199-236

[23] Eisenberger R, Huntington R, Hutchison S, Sowa D. Perceived organizational support. Journal of Applied Psychology. 1986;**71**:500-507

[24] Judge TA, Thoresen CJ, Bono JE, Patton GK. The job satisfaction – Job performance relationship: A qualitative and quantitative review. Psychological Bulletin. 2001;**127**:376-407

[25] Dalal RS. A meta-analysis of the relationship between organizational citizenship behavior and counterproductive workplace behavior. Journal of Applied Psychology. 2005;**90**:1241-1255

[26] Bies RJ, Tripp TM. The study of revenge in the workplace: Conceptual, ideological, and empirical issues. In: Fox S, Spector PE, editors. Counterproductive Work Behavior: Investigations of Actors and Targets. Washington, DC: American Psychological Association; 2005. pp. 65-81

[27] Manogran P, Stauffer J, Conlon EJ. Leader-member exchange as a key mediating variable between employees' perceptions of fairness and organizational citizenship behavior. In: Proceedings of the National Academy of Management Meeting. Dallas, TX: Pearson; 1994

[28] Moorman RH, Blakely GL, Niehoff BP. Does perceived organizational support mediate the relationship between procedural justice and organizational citizenship behavior? Academy of Management Journal. 1998;**41**:351-357

[29] Johnson JL, O'Leary-Kelly AM. The effects of psychological contract breach and organizational cynicism: Not all social exchange violations are created equal. Journal of Organizational Behavior. 2003;**24**:627-647

[30] Penny LM, Spector PE. Job stress, incivility and counterproductive workplace behavior [CWB]: The moderating role of negative affectivity. Journal of Organizational Behavior. 2005;**26**(5):777-796

[31] Spector PE. The role frustration in anti-social behavior at work. In: Giacalone RA, Greenberg J (Eds.), Anti-Social Behavior in Organizations. Thousand Oaks, CA, US: Sage Publication, Inc.; 1997. pp. 1-17

[32] Fontaine RG. Disentangling the psychology and of instrumental and reactive subtypes of aggression. Psychology, Public Policy and Law. 2007;**13**:143-165

[33] Bowling NA, Eschleman KJ. Employee personality as a moderator of the relationships between work stressors and counterproductive work behavior. Journal of Occupational Health Psychology. 2010;**15**(1):91-103

[34] Mount M, Ilies R, Johnson E. Relationship of personality traits and counterproductive workplace behaviors: The mediating effects of job satisfaction. Personnel Psychology. 2006;**59**(3):591-622

[35] Yang J, Diefendorff JM. The relationship of daily counterproductive workplace behaviors with emotions, situational antecedents and personality moderators: A diary study in Hongkong. Personnel Psychology. 2009;**62**(2):259-295

[36] Fida R, Paciello M, Tramontano C, Fontaine RG, Barbaranelli C, Farnese ML. An integrative approach to understanding counterproductive work behavior: The roles of stressors, negative emotions and moral disengagement. Journal of Business Ethics. 2015;**130**:131-144

[37] Hollensbe EC, Khazanchi S, Masterson SS. How do I assess if my supervisor and organization are fair? Identifying the rules underlying entity-based justice perceptions. Academy of Management Journal. 2008;**51**:1099-1116

[38] Kernan M, Hanges P. Survivor reactions to reorganization: Antecedents and consequences of procedural, interpersonal, and informational justice. Journal of Applied Psychology. 2002;**87**:916-928

[39] El Akremi A, Vandenberghe C, Camerman J. The role of justice and social exchange relationships in workplace deviance: Test of a mediated model. Human Relations. 2010;**63**(11):1687-1717

[40] Aquino K, Lewis MU, Bradfield M. Justice constructs, negative affectivity, and employee deviance: A proposed model and empirical test. Journal of Organizational Behavior. 1999;**20**(7):1073-1091

[41] Ambrose ML, Seabrigh MA, Schminke M. Sabotage in the workplace: The role of organizational injustice. Organizational Behavior and Human Decision Processes. 2002;**89**:947-965

[42] Chernyak-Hai L, Tziner A. Organizational citizenship behaviors [OCBs]: Socio-psychological antecedents and consequences. International Review of Social Psychology. 2012;**25**(3/4):53-92

[43] Karriker JH, Williams ML. Organizational justice and organizational citizenship behavior: A mediated multifocal model. Journal of Management. 2009;**35**:112-135

[44] Schulte M, Ostroff C, Kinicki AJ. Organizational climate systems and psychological climate perceptions: A cross-level study of climate-satisfaction relationships. Journal of Occupational and Organizational Psychology. 2006;**79**:645-671

[45] Ivancevitch JM, Konopaske R, Matteson MT. Organizational Behavior and Management. 6th ed. New York: McGraw-Hill/Irwin; 2008

[46] Martin KD, Cullen JB. Continuities and extensions of ethical climate theory: A meta-analytic review. Journal of Business Ethics. 2006;**69**:175-194

[47] Leung AS. Matching ethical work climate to in-role and extra-role behaviors in a collectivist work setting. Journal of Business Ethics. 2008;**79**(1-2):43-55

[48] Mayer DM, Kuenzi M, Greenbaum RL. Examining the link between ethical leadership and employee misconduct: The mediating role of ethical climate. Journal of Business Ethics. 2010;**95**(1):7-16

[49] Peterson D. The relationship between unethical behavior and the dimensions of the ethical climate questionnaire. Journal of Business Ethics. 2002;**41**:313-326

[50] Chernyak-Hai L, Tziner A. Relationships between counterproductive work behavior, perceived justice and climate, occupational status, and leader-member exchange. Journal of Work and Organizational Psychology. 2014;**30**(1):1-12

[51] Schein E. Organizational culture. Frankfurt: Campus Verlug; 1995

[52] Griffin RW, O'Leary-Kelly A. The Dark Side of Organizational Behavior. San Francisco: Jossev-Bass; 2004

[53] Al-Saudi MA. The impact of organizational climate upon the innovative behavior at Jordanian private universities as perceived by employees: A field study. International Business and Management. 2012;**5**(2):14-26

[54] Kidwell RE, Valentine SE. Positive group context, work attitudes, and organizational misbehavior. The case of withholding job effort. Journal of Business Ethics. 2009;**86**:15-28

[55] Appelbaum SH, Laconi GD, Matousek A. Positive and negative workplace behaviors. Causes, impacts, and solutions. Corporate Governance. 2007;**7**(5):586-598

[56] Adenike A. Organizational climate as a predictor of employee job satisfaction. Evidence from Covenant University. Business School Intelligence Journal. 2011;**4**(1):151-165

[57] Vigoda-Gadot E, Drory A. Handbook of Organizational Politics. Cheltenham, UK: Edward Elgar; 2006

[58] Mintzberg H. Power in and around Organizations. Eaglewood Cliffs, NJ: Prentice Hall; 1983

[59] Kacmar KM, Baron RA. Organizational politics: The state of the field, links to related processes, and an agenda for future research. In: Ferris GR, editor. Research in Personnel and Human Resources Management. Vol. 17. Stamford, CT: JAI Press; 1999. pp. 1-39

[60] Witt LA, Hochwarter, Kacmar KM. Perception of organizational politics as a moderator of the relationship between conscientious and job performance. Journal of Applied Psychology. 2000;**85**(3):472-478

[61] Ferris GR, Russ GS, Fandt PM. Politics in organizations. In: Giacalone RA, Rosenfeld P, editors. Impression Management in Organization. Hillsdale, NJ: Lawrence Erlbaum; 1989. pp. 143-170

[62] Andrews MC, Kacmar KM. Discriminating among organizational politics, justice and support. Journal of Organizational Behavior. 2001;**22**:347-357

[63] Kacmar KM, Carlson DS. Further validation of the perception of politics scale [POPS]: A multiple sample investigation. Journal of Management. 1997;**23**:627-660

[64] Ferris GR, Harrell-Cook G, Dulebohn J. Organizational politics: The nature of the relationship between politics perceptions and political behavior. Research in the Sociology of Organization. 2000;**17**:89-130

[65] Ferris GR, Adams G, Kolodinsky RW, Hochwarter WA, Ammeter AP. Perceptions of organizational politics: Theory and research directions. In: Yammarino FJ, Dansereau F, editors. The Many Faces Multi Level Issues. WY

London: Emerald Group Publishing; 2002. pp. 179-254

[66] Chang C, Rosen CC, Levy PE. The relationship between perception of organizational politics and employee attitude, strain and behavior: A meta-analytic examination. Academy of Management Journal. 2009;**52**(4):779-801

[67] Miller BK, Rutherford MA, Kolodinsky RW. Perception of organizational politics: A meta-analysis of outcomes. Journal of Business Psychology. 2008;**22**(3):209-222

[68] Penny LM, Spector PE. Emotion and counterproductive work behavior. In: Ashkanasy NM, Cooper CL, editors. Research Companion to Emotion in Organization. Cheltenham: Edward Elgar; 2008. pp. 138-196

[69] Pindek S, Spector PE. Organizational constraints: A meta-analysis of a major stressor. Work and Stress. 2016;**30**(1):7-25

[70] Fox S, Spector PE, Miles D. Counterproductive work behaviors [CWBs] in response to job stressors and organizational justice: Some mediator and moderator test for autonomy and emotions. Journal of Vocational Behavior. 2001;**59**(3):291-309

[71] Mitchell MS, Ambrose ML. Abusive supervision and workplace deviance and the moderating effects of negative reciprocity beliefs. Journal of Applied Psychology. 2007;**92**(4):1159-1168

[72] Ferris GR, Frink DD, Galang MC, Xhou J, Kacmar MK, Howard JI. Perception of organizational politics: Predictions, stress-related implications and outcome. Human Relations. 1996;**49**(2):233-266

[73] Vigoda-Gadot E. Stress-related aftermaths to workplace politics, job distress and aggressive behavior in organizations. Journal of Organizational Behavior. 2002;**23**(5):571-591

[74] Wiltshire J, Bourdage J, Lee K. Honesty-humility and perception of organizational politics in predicting workplace outcomes. Journal of Business Psychology. 2014;**29**(2):235-251

[75] Zettler I, Hilbig BE. Honesty-humility and a person-situation interaction at work. European Journal of Personality. 2010;**24**(7):569-582

[76] Meisler G, Drory A, Vigoda-Gadot E. Perceived organizational politics and counterproductive work behavior: The mediating role of hostility. Personnel Review. 2020;**49**(8):1506-1517

[77] Bauer TN, Green SG. The development of leader-member exchange: A longitudinal test. Academy of Management Journal. 1996;**39**:1538-1567

[78] Gouldner AW. The norm of reciprocity: A preliminary statement. American Sociological Review. 1960;**25**(2):161-178

[79] Kelloway EK, Sivanathan N, Francis L, Barling J. Poor leadership. In: Barling J, Kelloway EK, Frone M, editors. Handbook of Workplace Stress. Sage Publication; 2005. pp. 89-112

[80] Dulebohn JH, Bommer WH, Liden RC, Brouer RL, Ferris GR. A meta-analysis of antecedents and consequences of leader-member exchange. Integrating the past with an eye towards the future. Journal of Management. 2012;**38**(6):1715-1759

[81] Martin R, Guillaume Y, Thomas G, Lee A, Epitropaki O. Leader-member exchange (LMX) and performance: A meta-analytic review. Personnel Psychology. 2016;**69**(1):67-121

[82] Tziner A, Fein E, Oren L. Human motivation and performance outcomes

in the context of downsizing. In: Cooper CL, Pandey A, Quick JC, editors. Downsizing: Is less Still More? 1st ed. Cambridge, UK: Cambridge University Press; 2012. pp. 103-133

[83] Zaccaro SJ, Ely K, Nelson J. Leadership processes and work motivation. In: Kanfer R, Chen G, Pritchard RD, editors. Work Motivation: Past, Present, and Future. New York: Routledge; 2008. pp. 319-360

[84] Ilies R, Nahrgang JD, Morgeson FP. Leader-member exchange and citizenship behaviors: A meta-analysis. Journal of Applied Psychology. 2007;**92**(1):269-277

[85] de Oliveira LB, de Assis V, Jr de Moreno VA, Gonçalves RC. Individual and situational antecedents of CWBs. Brazilian Administration Review. 2020;**17**(3):1-21

[86] Newton C, Perlow R. The role of leader-member exchange relations and individual differences on CWB. Psychological Report. 2021:1-37

[87] Holtz BC, Harold CM. Effects of leadership consideration and structure on employee perceptions of justice and counterproductive work behavior. Journal of Organizational Behavior. 2013;**34**(4):492-519

[88] Roberts BW. Back to the future: Personality and assessment and personality development. Journal of Research in Personality. 2009;**43**(2):137-145

[89] Salgado JF. The big five personality dimensions and counterproductive behaviors. International Journal of Selection and Assessment. 2002;**10**(1-2):117-125

[90] Spector PE. The relationship of personality to counterproductive work behavior [CWB]: An integration of perspectives. Human Resource Management Review. 2011;**21**(4):342-352

[91] Lazarus RS. Cognition and motivation in emotion. American Psychologist. 1991a;**46**(4):352-367

[92] Lazarus RS. Progress on a cognitive-motivational-relational theory of emotion. American Psychologist. 1991b;**46**(8):819-834

[93] Bolton LR, Becker LK, Barber LK. Big five trait predictors of differential counterproductive work behavior dimensions. Personality and Individual Differences. 2010;**49**:537-541

[94] Waheeda S, Hafidz M. Individual differences as antecedents of CWBs. Asian Social Science. 2012;**8**(13):220-226

[95] Lee JA, Soutar G. Is Schwartz's value survey an internal scale, and does it really matter. Journal of Cross-Cultural Psychology. 2010;**41**(1):76-86

[96] Morselli D, Spini D, Devos T. Human values and trust in institutions across countries: A multilevel test of Schwartz's hypothesis of structural equivalence. Survey Research Methods. 2012;**6**(1):49-60

[97] Braithwaite VA, Blamey R. Consensus, stability and meaning in abstract social values. Australian Journal of Political Science. 1998;**33**:363-380

[98] Schwartz SH. Universals in the content and structure of values: Theory and empirical tests in 20 countries. In: Zanna M, editor. Advances in Experimental Social Psychology. Vol. 25. New York: Academic Press; 1992. pp. 1-65

[99] Bruursema K. How Individual Values and Trait Boredom Interface with Job Characteristics and Job Boredom in their Effects on CWB [Doctoral Dissertation]. Available from: ProQuest Dissertations and Theses database database. [UMI No. 3260044]. Tampa, FL: University of Florida; 2007

[100] Paulhus DL, Williams KM. The dark triads of personality: Narcissism, Machiavellianism, and psychopath. Journal of Resources Personality. 2002;**36**:556-563

[101] Smith SF, Lilienfeld SO. Psychopath in the workplace: The known and unknowns. Aggressive Violent Behavior. 2013;**18**:204-218

[102] Barlett CP. Exploring the correlations between emerging adulthood, dark triad traits, and aggressive behavior. Personality of Individual Differences. 2016;**101**:293-298

[103] Geel M, van Geomans A, Toprak F, Wedder P. Which personality trait is related to bullying and cyber-bullying? A study with the big five, dark triads and sadism. Personality of Individual Differences. 2017;**106**:231-235

[104] Palmer JC, Komarraju M, Carter MZ, Karau SJ. Angel on one shoulder: Can perceived organizational support moderate the relationship between the dark triad traits and counterproductive work behavior? Personality of Individual Differences. 2017;**110**:31-37

[105] O'Boyle EH, Forsyth DR, Banks GC, McDaniel MA. A meta-analysis of the dark triads and work behavior: A social exchange perspective. Journal of Applied Psychology. 2012;**97**:557-579

[106] Grijalva E, Newman DA. Narcissism and CWBs: Meta-analysis and consideration of collectivist culture, big five personality and narcissism's facet structure. Applied Psychology. 2014;**64**:93-126

[107] Wu J, Lebreton JM. Reconsidering the dispositional basis of CWB: The role of aberrant personality. Personal Psychology. 2011;**64**:593-626

[108] Hare RD, Neuman CS. Psychopath: Assessment and forensic implication. Canadian Journal of Psychiatry. 2009;**54**:791-802

[109] Scherer KT, Baysinger M, Zolysnky D, LeBreton JM. Predicting CWBs with sub-clinical psychopath. Beyond the five factor model of personality. Personality of Individual Differences. 2013;**55**:300-305

[110] Baloch MA, Meng F, Xu Z, Cepeda-Carrion ID, Bari MW. Dark triads, perception of organizational politics and CWBs: The moderating effect of political skills. Frontiers in Psychology. 2017;**8**(1972):1-14

[111] Spector PE. The relationship of personality to CWBs: An integration of perspectives. Human Resources Management Review. 2010;**21**:342-252

[112] Penny LM, Spector PE. Narcissism and CWBs: Do bigger egos mean bigger problems? International Journal of Selection and Assessment. 2002;**10**:126-134

[113] Kish-Gephart JJ, Harrison DA, Trevino LK. Bad apples, bad cases and bad barrels: Meta-analytic evidence about sources of unethical decisions at work. Journal of Applied Psychology. 2010;**95**:1-31

[114] Harris LC, Ogbonna E. Service sabotage: A study of antecedents and consequences. Journal of the Academy of Marketing Science. 2006;**34**(4):543-558

[115] Vatankhah S, Darvishi M. Unpacking solution to CWBs using hybrid fuzzy MCDM. The Service Industries Journal. 2021;**42**(3):1-28. DOI: 10.1080/02642069.2021.2012164

Chapter 5

Why Fear Crushes Your Culture

Mary Clare Coghlan, Andrew B. Ross and Mia B. Russell

Abstract

Fear is defined as a normal reaction to a real or imagined threat and is an integral and adaptive aspect of development. Individuals react to fear during moments of social, political, and economic upheaval like those in recent years. But how do *collective groups* manifest and respond to the internal and external factors that promote fear? More pointedly, how do working professionals experience a long-term, organizational culture of fear? To respond to these questions, this chapter will offer new perspectives on how fear is operationalized in the workplace. By interpreting the role of fear in common workplace norms like feedback, collaboration, management, and hiring, we offer a better understanding of how organizational culture might promote the negative consequences of fear: avoidance, withdrawal, and physical/ emotional pain.

Keywords: culture, work, fear, feedback, trust, psychological safety

1. Introduction

It is common for an individual—as experienced as they might be—to feel a sense of nervous excitement walking into work on the first day of a new job. Many workers wake up on the day of an important meeting or high-stakes presentation feeling an acute worry gnawing at their confidence. These are familiar emotions, no matter what industry or social context an individual works within. They might even be reasonably viewed as part of the "everyday fabric" of contemporary work—the quotidian grievances and awkward anxieties that workplace sitcoms tend to use for comedic effect.

But beyond laughable clichés, there's nothing funny about the presence of intense or overwhelming fear at work, particularly in the context of negative outcomes for workers and employers alike. These feelings, which transcend the minor strains refenced above, can be intense and distressing, leaving emotional scarring and unease that can last for months or even years. These fears can be the source or symptom of traumatizing challenges that leave work a social context to dread and avoid.

While it is difficult to pin down what exactly qualifies as "fear," it is easy to see and experience instances in which the manifestations of this emotional response appear in the workplace. All workplaces have what Barsade & O'Neill call "an emotional culture"—the shared psychology of a group collaborating together on various aims [1]. Such "shared affective values, norms, artifacts, and assumptions" underpin the way that people experience meaning and satisfaction at work, or, on the other hand, how they experience negative emotional states that leave them feeling ambivalent about their work accomplishments [1].

Reasons for fear are ubiquitous—constant warnings about terrorism, international conflict, weakening economies, global warming, crime, infectious disease, and political uncertainty—cause a feeling of trepidation to pervade contemporary life. The social fabric of fear is visible in how groups perceive others, act in response to risk and uncertainty, and even bond together through shared distress. Fear shapes organizational culture in many aspects, as workers' relationships with their colleagues and leaders are often formed around real and perceived fears about power dynamics in the workplace. Companies might act strategically out of a fearful disposition—holding the line against an assumed threat that may not materialize. Running through a work culture of fear are fractures that divide and disable the collaborative relationships and meaningful well-being that organizations require to be successful.

On the individual level, neuroscientists often frame the emotion of fear in its most general sense as a psychological response to a perceived threat—what Joseph LeDoux has called "a conscious awareness that you are in harm's way" [2]. Such a response manifests itself biologically (sweating, rapid heartbeat, eye movement, etc.) and cognitively, as in racing thoughts or a kind of frozen panic. These individual responses often remain private and even suppressed, as such manifestations of distress tend to be perceived as inappropriate or off-putting in a professional context.

Whether visibly manifested or not, fear is "at work" in the lives of many employees, managers, and participants in the complex social dance that is work. While fear is certainly not a strictly-contemporary phenomenon (one has only to think of the dangers of many nineteenth-century pre-reform workplaces to consider the ubiquity of workplace anxiety) there is good reason to carefully study the role it plays in today's world of work. Even in the global "knowledge economy", where work is more distributed and digital than ever before, new fears arise that need to be considered for their social, economic, and psychological implications. Understanding how fear is *operationalized* through key workplace norms will reveal psychological barriers to productivity and meaning-making at work. Such analysis also lay foundational principles and practices for reducing and reframing fear.

We begin this chapter by defining fear as a psychological phenomenon that manifests at work and summarizing how several generations of researchers in organizational psychology and behavior management disciplines have understood the impact of fear on employees and managers alike. The chapter then applies this research to one common workplace norm by considering feedback as an essential activity that is nevertheless deeply shaped by fear and the way that it limits trust. To conclude, the chapter presents the concept of psychological safety as a response to workplace fear, drawing on two examples from well-known corporations to understand the potential of this key principle.

2. Literature review

Fear is a human emotion that is activated automatically and typically very quickly. Conceptualized as an affective state protecting one against danger or a motivational state leading one away from something, fear yields a reaction to an immediate threat—that can be physical, emotional, or psychological—and may be directed to external sources. An example of a physical reaction might include sweating palms whereas an emotional reaction may emerge as worry and rumination. Further, a psychological reaction may be indicated by an upset stomach or nervous jitters.

As a type of emotion, fear, an intervening variable, is closely related to stimulus events as well as response events. Fear encourages avoidance behavior, a narrowed perceptual and cognitive focus on and pessimistic judgment about risks and the future. Fear is a driver of action—not only psychological but also physical as our body kicks into overdrive. In other words, fear motivates withdrawal and avoidance of harmful events. Additionally, fear has been considered a relational construct, aroused in response to a situation that is judged as dangerous and toward which protective action should be taken. From this perspective, fear shaped human behavior and it continues to do so today.

Fear can be explained through protection motivation theory. Drawing from previous research by Lazarus, Rogers sought to better understand fear appeals and how people cope with them [3]. Protection motivation theory (PMT) centers on three critical components: the magnitude of noxiousness of a depicted event, probability of that event's occurrence, and efficacy of a protective response [3]. PMT proposes that people protect themselves from fear based on two factors: threat appraisal and coping appraisal. Threat appraisal assesses the severity of the situation and examines how serious the situation is, while coping appraisal explains the response to the situation. These processes mediate attitude change—in other words, these processes help explain how the emotion of fear motivates action.

Fear, in particular, evolved to protect us against threats to our survival, and its evolutionary-based effects continue to influence us despite the changed nature of the threats we face [4]. Since the average person spends approximately one-third of their waking hours at work, it is safe to assume that work-related fear can in periods also be a significant influence upon the general well-being of individuals. At work, fear can be seen through physiological and emotional responses, as well as those that are relational and interpersonal. Fear is also manifested through organizational action—collective manifestations of fear with company- and market-wide effects. Researchers have tracked fear at work as manifested through feelings and behavior related to insecurity, avoidance, as well as a lack of psychological safety and trust. Gibaldi & Cusack sought to understand the factors and conditions that make employees fearful [5]. They found the following sources of fear that people experience in their daily work lives: fear of reprisal, reprimand, making mistakes, failure, giving voice/speaking up, termination, and feedback among others [6].

Fear is psychological but it has physical effects as well. Stress and anxiety resulting from workplace fear can cause increased heart rate, sweating, adrenaline rush and even a fight or flight response. Fear spreads from the mind to the body. This feeling often leads to employees being paralyzed with fear and unable to work effectively. An individual that is experiencing fear may have an increased heart rate, faster breathing, shortness of breath, digestive changes, sweating, chills, or even trembling muscles. Adrenaline and cortisol flood our system, we breathe faster and our blood flows away from our hearts and into our limbs. Our body is preparing for "fight or flight" [7]. In addition, from a physiological and emotional lens, fear may manifest as fatigue, irritability, negative attitude and affect, frustration, indecisiveness, loss of confidence, forgetfulness, and rumination. Perhaps you have seen an employee that is present, but only in the physical sense—not bringing their best selves to work and not fully contributing. Fear may also be evident in the way that employees work together, collaborate, and compete. Some individuals experience fear leading to fatigue—a 2019 ComPsych Survey showed that 61% of workers reported a high level of stress that caused fatigue and feelings of not being in control [8]. Though fearful, out-of-control feelings may be intense in the short term, such exhaustion-inducing stresses can also be paralyzing over a significant time period [9].

Beyond being an individual inevitability, it is important to recognize that fear in the workplace is an organizational problem for both employers and employees, making a workplace uncomfortable (or even intolerable). Fear can also have a negative impact on revenue, profits, and other metrics of success. A constant state of fear negatively impacts an employee's ability to speak their mind, admit a mistake, or feel safe giving honest feedback. This can cause employees and companies alike to make decisions from a place *to not lose* instead of *to win*. In fact, previous research by O'Donovan discusses competition as a useful mechanism for creativity and innovation within an organization as well as an instrument of repression as employees are sometimes pitted against one another [10]. For individuals, the stress of competition can be physically and psychologically destructive leading to lower morale and reduced productivity. In this way, competition harms the levels of inter-communication of ideas, coordination of efforts, friendliness and pride in the group, and ultimately the level of harmony and cohesion in the group [11]. Perhaps unsurprisingly, competition that breeds rivalry has been suggested to lead to the development of negative interdependence, distrust, lack of harmony, and opportunistic behavior that prioritizes self-interests over collective interests [11, 12].

What's worse is that there is a great concern in the sense that fear is contagious and can travel quickly throughout an organization. And this contagion helps to foster a culture of fear whereas individuals *catch* the emotions of others. This emotional *catching* process is better described as a cognitive, either nonconscious or conscious, process of emotional contagion where people imagine how they would feel in the position of another and, consequently, experience the same feelings. Other costs that organizations bear include low employee morale, reduced productivity, and high employee turnover. The costs of rampant workplace fear create a significant incentive to ameliorate this condition. In the current context of work, these conditions can lead to devastating financial costs for a business and require that leaders and organizations protect against a culture of fear.

3. Fear of feedback

Rather than speculating about external social forces like natural disasters or political disruptions and their influence on individuals' perceptions of their workplace safety, we choose to focus on one internal workplace norm that is common across sectors and roles: feedback. As a workplace norm that most if not all employees experience, feedback is a particularly valuable case study for understanding potential reasons and effects of psychological unease at work.

Just as it is challenging to generalize a conclusive list of ways that individuals might experience fear at work, it is difficult to narrowly define work-related feedback—it is a complex social dynamic. Even defining this activity as "language used for the purpose of assessing and improving behavior" overlooks the reality that much feedback can be nonverbal, presented in the form of gestures, looks, or even silence. Definitions of feedback as "a reinforcer," "an instruction," or "a guide" are often tempered with caveats about the malleability of feedback practices and their application across different work environments (see [13] for a helpful review of "behavior analytic" definitions of feedback). In one influential essay, Peterson even went so far as to argue that "feedback" should be abandoned by behavior analysists as a term, arguing that in its universal ambiguity the term has become nothing more than "professional slang" [14].

Even though it may be difficult to unambiguously define, feedback has remained one of the most widely-studied functional motivational practices in the organizational behavior management literature [15, 16]. Even Peterson's general critique of the term includes an underlying assumption of its potential: that analysis can improve feedback to be maximally effective for changing behavior as an "effective conditioned reinforcer, or a discriminative stimulus, or an establishing stimulus" [14]. Feedback offers employees directed motivation and improved overall job satisfaction [17]. In particular, research indicates that satisfaction with feedback is likely to improve workers' commitment to their organization and decrease the likelihood of employee turnover [18].

The research literature on this topic has generally focused on the benefits of feedback. What is less well-understood is the psychological intensity and the deeply-held feelings of fear that accompany this workplace norm. In other words, while there seems to be ample research evidence to feedback's overall benefits, much less is understood then about the demotivating fears that accompany feedback or prevent feedback from happening in an organization. How does fear inform professionals' view of evaluation? And how do professionals experience fear in the moment of providing or receiving feedback? These two questions focus both on mindset and behavior—they seek to understand the mechanics of feedback fear, avoidance, and general negativity and to clarify the disfunctions that arise in fear-based work environments.

Some individuals may look forward to the direction that evaluation from supervisors provides. In fact, some research indicates that some individuals reported negative or corrective feedback as being more valuable over positive response, in part due to the way that it helps recipients improve more efficiently [19]. Another way of understanding the influence of fear in the context of feedback is to suggest that most people see this workplace norm as a "necessary evil" or "bitter pill"—an experience that holds benefits but is in large measure to be endured, not enjoyed. This negative perception of feedback fosters a culture of fear around feedback, as individuals' relationship with feedback tends to feed off of each other. As Jackman & Strober argue, this amplification of fears over feedback often results in the organizational equivalent of "psychologically maladaptive behaviors such as procrastination, denial, brooding, jealousy, and self-sabotage" [20].

Fear, as a response to a psychologically straining stimulus perceived as being uncontrollable, can be experienced in an anticipatory mode in the context of feedback. This is especially true when feedback is framed as an antecedent to change [13, 14]. A sense of dread is often present for individuals' in advance of their either giving or receiving feedback—an anticipatory anxiety over the likelihood of conflict, embarrassment, or mis-characterization. This can be as true for the giver of feedback, as for the receiver; therefore, much feedback is never given at all due to the anticipated likelihood of creating a strained or awkward relationship with a managed colleague or employee. To offset this negative outcome, several researchers have recommended that feedback be iterative and frequent, becoming a practice that is consistent and expected [21–24].

"Fear during" (as in a more immediate or of-the-moment phenomenon) is also present in the feedback scenario. Recipients' emotional response to feedback in the moment may in part be due to the cultural valences of words commonly used while giving feedback (i.e., "excellent" or "ineffective") that carry psychosocial associations and even physiological responses [16]. These responses can be especially present during evaluative feedback, as in the case of the annual review. Research has shown that these situations are as psychologically challenging for managers as they are for employees, largely due to the perceived likelihood that an employee would respond negatively to the feedback [25]. In addition to increasing the chance of over-rating or being lenient with employees [26], this management anxiety can corrode trust within organizations [27]. In response, some have argued that correctives to the anxiety surrounding performance appraisal are to present the manager less as a judge and more as a coach or servant [28] and to build in additional iterations of feedback outside of an annual or more isolated review [25].

One somewhat surprising outcome of fear of feedback is that many professionals never request or receive feedback from supervisors or colleagues. By understanding the negative inputs that inform the experience of feedback, including the anxieties that motivate the avoidance of feedback, researchers can better understand the way that productive dialog is hindered from fear-based psychosocial drivers. This understanding has implications for leadership development training, as well as for understanding the psychology and culture of professional organizations—everything from corporate, education, medical, and even athletic contexts.

4. Trust

Effective feedback is not possible in the absence of trust, in part because it's truly challenging for an individual to listen in an "open" way to feedback given by someone they do not trust or respect. On the other hand, evaluative feedback that is perceived as being accurate and offered in a spirit of genuine goodwill is likely to improve trust between managers and their employees [17]. Organizations are defined by the sum of their parts; and the foundation of the social cohesion that holds them together is supported by trust, safety, and respect. Yet when an organization fosters a culture of fear, critical factors—trust, accountability, safety, and respect—are all too often the casualties. Similarly, when negative feedback arises, research suggests that teams that have not established meaningful trust are more likely to see this feedback as indicative of unavoidable failure and are especially likely to experience major team conflict [29].

Trust is foundational in all relationships, including the employment relationship. Organizations with high levels of intra-group trust have been shown to be more likely to avoid the pitfalls of conflict and divisiveness that hinder important workplace collaborations [30]. When employees feel that their leader is not trustworthy, safety and trust diminish [31]. Trustworthiness is built from three factors: ability, benevolence, and integrity. If employees perceive their leader as competent, honest, and benevolent—or interested in their overall well-being, as a person who can help in the task or relationship, and as possessing integrity, they will feel safe and will be less likely to engage in self-protective defenses at work. In fact, transparency and vulnerability in relationships between leaders and employees contribute to both a feeling of efficacy and clarity that drives fear out of the relationship [32]. These types of high-quality relationships breed collegiality, productive conflict, trust, and psychological safety.

5. Psychological safety

In her article, "Psychological safety and learning behavior in work teams," Amy Edmondson defines "psychological safety" as a shared belief that the team is safe for interpersonal risk-taking [33]. It means that colleagues, regardless of who is sitting around the table, can share their ideas without judgment. The culture cultivated in teams with high psychological safety is one where people feel obligated, not fearful, to be candid.

In 2015, researcher Julia Rozovsky and her team were assigned by Google's "People Operations Department" to Project Aristotle, a long-term study on team effectiveness- named for Aristotle's belief that a team is greater than the sum of its parts [34]. The researchers first examined what distinguished a "team" from a work group, determining that the former is highly interdependent—a team needs each other to get work done [35]. Next, effectiveness was measured in four ways: executive evaluation of the team, team leader evaluation of the team, team member evaluation of the team, sales performance against quarterly quota [35]. Rozovsky's team conducted over 200 interviews with Google employees and looked at more than 250 attributes of over 180 Google teams and concluded that there are 5 dynamics of high-performing teams: *psychological safety, dependability, structure and clarity, meaning of work and impact of work* [36]. Psychological safety is an individual's perception of taking an interpersonal risk, teams high in this are confident they will not be embarrassed or judged [35]. Dependability is about counting on teammates to do high quality work on time [35]. Structure and clarity are when goals, roles, and execution plans are clear [35]. The meaning of work is experienced when people feel their work is personally meaningful, drawing reasons which can vary among the team [35]. The impact of work is when there is a subjective judgment that an individual's work is making a team fundamentally believe that the work they do matters [35]. Rozovsky's team found that psychological safety was not just by far the most important of the five key dynamics, it was also the underpinning of the other four [36]. Teams with high psychological safety are not only less likely to develop interpersonal conflicts, they are also more likely to admit mistakes, to collaborate, to take on new roles and more likely to harness the power of diverse ideas [36]. Rozovsky's conclusions are not simply predictors of improved contentment among colleagues; psychologically safe teams make more money and are rated twice as effective by executives [36].

Edmonson is very clear about what psychological safety is not: it is not about being nice or lowering standards. Psychological safety is about the climate of the team atmosphere; there is a focus on the personality of team more than any individual. Although trust is a part of psychological safety, Edmondson warns there are a few distinctions to be made. The first is that trust is between individuals where psychological safety is about a team. The second is that psychological safety is about mutual respect; people can be themselves. Creating a place where people can be themselves does not mean it is a place without accountability or standards. Lastly, trust is something that can indicate future actions—one may "trust" that their colleagues are going to do what they say they are going to do while psychological safety focuses on the moment, such as when one admits to a mistake or presents an unconventional idea in a discussion. We can see that psychological safety is defined by trust and respect but also by standards of excellence [37].

5.1 Why a lack of psychological safety hurts the culture

Rozovsky found that taking a risk around your team would be something simple, but she asks her readers to reflect on team experiences and how employees and team members err on the side of "playing it safe" for self-protection [36]. She states that individuals are reluctant to engage in behaviors that can negatively influence how others perceive their competence [36]. An individual might choose to not ask a clarifying question, or avoid challenging their boss with a different strategy because they fear negative judgment and retribution. This is only emphasized in hierarchies where the most influential and loudest voices are at the top. Research in neuroscience shows that fear consumes physiological resources, diverting them from parts of the brain that manage working memory and process new information [37]. This in turn impairs analytic thinking, creative insight, and problem solving. So not only is learning inhibited by fear but it also creates obstacles to asking for help and trying new things. Edmondson states it also affects employee satisfaction, hierarchy specifically, the fear it creates when not handled well, reduces psychological safety. Research shows that lower-status team members generally feel less safe than higher-status members as we are constantly assessing our relative status, monitoring how we stack up against others, again mostly subconsciously. Further, those lower in the status hierarchy experience stress in the presence of those with higher status [37].

Rozovsky and Edmondson highlight that psychological safety is imperative for effective teams and successful organizations. Two case studies will demonstrate the impact of psychological safety's presence and absence.

5.2 Volkswagen

Volkswagen, a globally-recognized German automotive company founded in 1937 had a 2022 revenue of $295.7B and assets of $638B [38]. In 2015, in a scandal called "diesel dupe", the United States Environmental Protection Agency reported that Volkswagen cars sold in America featured software known as "defeat devices" that could detect when they were being tested for emissions and subsequently change their performance to pass the tests. Over 480,000 cars in the U.S. featured these "devices," workarounds that allowed emissions over forty times above standard regulations. Volkswagen eventually admitted that about 11 million cars worldwide were fitted with defeat devices [39].

How could a company with so much capital not start over but rather risk its reputation? Would not it appear inefficient to spend time cheating and risking fines? There was a massive marketing campaign in the United States that was touting low-emitting vehicles and this led to pressure that fostered an environment not where people felt safe to say they needed to start over to comply with the regulations but instead to cheat around them [39]. The resulting controversy has damaged Volkswagen's reputation and financial standing as a major player in the automotive industry. In 2020, the company was fined upwards of $25B with not only more expected but also indictments of senior executives, including charges for the CEO, Martin Wilterkorn, in the U.S. and Germany. Volkswagen recalled 8.5 million cars in Europe, including 2.4 million in Germany, 1.2 million in the UK, and 500,000 in the U.S. [39]. How did a lack of psychological safety cause this automotive giant to post its first quarterly loss in 15 years of $2.6B? [39].

As all information of "diesel dupe" came to fruition, it was clear that top-level officials were insistent on the cheating to happen and that the company culture lacked space for people to share their concerns or even to collaborate on ideas to fix a long-term problem. As CEO Winterkorn was, in the words of one journalist, "a notorious micromanager—he was known for carrying a micrometer with him, so he could personally measure VW parts and tolerances down to the hundredth of a millimeter—and an imperious martinet" [40]. Reuters interviewed five former VW executives that told of a management style under Winterkorn that fostered a climate of fear and authoritarianism that went unchecked partly due to a company structure. Professor Ferdinand Dudenhöffer, automotive expert at the University of Duisburg-Essen, shared that the culture and organizational structure of Volkswagen are not comparable to other German automotive companies, such as Daimler or BMW, and that employees at Volkswagen talked of a special pressure [41]. In a *New York Times* article, David Bach, of Yale School of Management, concluded that Volkswagen became a place where subordinates were not only fearful of contradicting their superiors but also afraid to admit failure which he attributes to a self-righteousness [42]. Emanuela Montefrancesco, a Volkswagen engineer, described a hard-charging work culture where highly educated and motivated engineers competed for approval and promotion culture, too often failing to stand up to say: "I won't do this. I cannot. I am sorry" [42]. Such reticence to voice disagreement and thereby risk retribution indicates a lack of psychological safety at Volkswagen.

The new Volkswagen Chief Executive, Herbert Diess, plans to use more transparency, a more open culture of discussion, more accountability, and greater tolerance of errors [43]. You can simply look at Volkswagen's current website "The Foundations of The Group's Values", which illustrates their desire to cultivate Diess' desired culture. The first three values listed are *responsibility, honesty and bravery* [44]. *Responsibility* is defined by taking on social responsibility and paying attention to the environmental compatibility of the products and processes and dedication to improving them. *Honesty* is by doing the right thing when no one is watching, highlighting that they are not afraid of hierarchies and to share thoughts openly. *Bravery* demonstrates a focus on letting go and thinking afresh [44]. We can connect this articulation of Volkswagen's values to Edmondson's definition of psychological safety: interpersonal risk taking, sharing ideas without judgment, and a place where people are not fearful of being candid [33]. Volkswagen is searching to cultivate what they so deeply lacked before: *psychological safety.*

5.3 Pixar

Pixar Animation Studio, an American computer animation studio and successful subsidiary of The Walt Disney Company, released its first movie, *Toy Story*, in 1995 and has grossed more than $14.7B globally [45]. In creative environments, which are demanding and high stakes, there needs to be a high quantity of ideas presented in order to have a blockbuster. CEO Ed Catmull cultivates a culture of transparency and feedback—benchmarks of psychological safety. Psychological safety is the antidote to fear and essential for creative environments. In order to come across an industry changing idea, there needs to be several ideas.

Catmull believes that in a fear-based, failure-averse culture, people will avoid risk, whether consciously or unconsciously. In this type of environment, innovative work cannot take place. One approach or remedy is to have leaders talk about mistakes which then makes it safe for others to do so. In his book, *Creativity, Inc.*, Catmull explains that "in a fearless culture, (or as fearless as nature will allow), people will be much less hesitant to explore new areas, identifying uncharted pathways and then charging them down" which allows them to be decisive and know when to reboot [46]. Catmull believes the hallmark of a healthy creative culture is that its people feel free to share ideas, opinions, and criticisms. That decision-making is better when teams draw upon the collective knowledge and unvarnished opinions of the group. He states that candor is the key to collaborating effectively [46]. Lack of candor leads to dysfunctional environments. So how can a manager ensure that his or her working group, department, or company embraces candor? Catmull has integrated two feedback concepts at Pixar that are glowing examples of psychological safety in action:

"the Braintrust" which takes place before a script is finalized and "postmortem" which takes place after a film is released.

Pixar relies on a candor-based mechanism known internally as "the Braintrust" to push each other toward excellence and away from mediocrity. Catmull describes this institutional practice as "our primary delivery system for straight talk. Braintrust meets every few months or so to assess each movie we're making. Its premise is simple: put smart, passionate people in a room together, charge them with identifying and solving problems, and encourage them to be candid. The Braintrust is not foolproof, but when we get it right, the results are phenomenal" [47]. Catmull is adamant this feedback system is different for two reasons—the group is composed of people who have been through the creative storytelling process themselves, and there is no hierarchical authority [46]. Unlike at Volkswagen, Pixar directors are able to independently determine the feedback they take—nothing is mandated. Catmull stresses the importance that candor is only valuable if the person is willing to hear it [46].

The trajectory of a film production changes multiple times over many years. In a high stress and high production environment, people move onto their next projects once a film is completed. But Catmull believes that at Pixar, "postmortems" are crucial for exploration of what did and did not work, and that companies, like individuals, do not become exceptional by believing they are exceptional but by understanding the ways in which they are not exceptional [46]. When teams are in the middle of production, it is hard to think about lessons learned from the process. Postmortems provide opportunities for those, both people embedded in the process and those on the outside, to get a high-level view on takeaways from the experience. Postmortems indicate that a commitment to transparent feedback does not just help motivate creativity, it also creates a safe place where personal frustrations can be shared so that resentment is not carried into other projects [46].

While Volkswagen is working to cultivate a culture where people will take employee feedback to innovate instead of succumbing to pressure to cheat, Pixar's culture of psychological safety is seen throughout their entire process. Pixar does not only emphasize the importance of feedback during the production cycle with Braintrust but also works to capture post-production learning lessons in postmortems, which would allow project team members, and others, to play a part in honest feedback. This focus on psychological safety multiple times in a project cycle normalizes feedback and gives employees the ability to take learning lessons into future projects. This success is demonstrated in some of the world's greatest movies such as *Toy Story, Frozen and Finding Nemo*—of which each had improvements to the initial script. These case studies demonstrate the negative impact of fear and its antidote: *psychological safety*.

6. Conclusion

We cannot escape this fact: fear is simply a part of life. While perhaps unavoidable, it is evident that the many contributory fear factors can be managed. Leaders and organizations control the conditions within the workplace that wreak havoc on employees. This control begets responsibility; a responsibility to reduce fear at work and to build psychological safety for their teams and organization. Leaders who express anger, frustration, and impatience may drive their employees into states of fear and survival. The dynamic twenty-first century workplace requires that we not only recognize and understand the role of fear but that we also work to overcome the embedded culture of fear that many organizations seemingly embrace. We have shown that though fear may be unavoidable, it is worth actively managing organizational culture. Specifically, leaders can embrace psychological safety, encourage effective feedback, and implement best practices that support learning and growth (for both employees and the organization). Candor, creativity, and reflective transparency can help to establish norms that work against the fears that contemporary workplace conditions often breed.

This chapter offers perspective on some of the norms that are both drivers of fear and driven by fear-based assumptions that employees and managers bring to work. Giving and receiving feedback is often feared. But we have argued that it is also essential—without the trust necessary to evaluate and assess each other, colleagues are unlikely to develop the psychological safety that makes teams and organizations successful. Similarly, fear at work not only minimizes the likelihood of "success" in terms of raw productivity, it (perhaps more importantly) diminishes the likelihood of work being meaningful for employees. In other words, fear inflicts avoidance, withdrawal, and emotional pains that negate the potential fulfillment of work.

While we have focused on feedback and psychological safety as key factors in understanding the role of fear at work, there are many other avenues and cases that need additional research. For instance, the COVID-19 pandemic and its associated destabilization of life provides a tremendous case study for illuminating the antecedents and consequences of fear in the workplace. Future research should include more nuanced measures of employee well-being in the immediate context of workplace fear: how do workers offset or counterbalance fear factors that jeopardize their well-being? The study of fear in the context of organizational behavior also stands to benefit from better understanding how and why organizations collectively act out of fear, or even the impact of cumulative fear on corporations' public perception, business strategy, and longevity in the market. Better understanding how fear informs individuals' and groups' experiences at work can generate opportunities for improving the workplace for all. As an antidote to fear, we recommend further study and implementation of psychological safety as a concept and practice.

Author details

Mary Clare Coghlan*, Andrew B. Ross and Mia B. Russell
Johns Hopkins University, Center for Leadership Education, Baltimore, MD, USA

*Address all correspondence to: mcoghla2@jhu.edu

References

[1] Barsade S, O'Neill OA. Manage your emotional culture. Harvard Business Review. 2016;**2016**:58-66

[2] Mobbs D, Adolphs R, Fanselow MS, Barrett LF, LeDoux JE, Ressler K, et al. Viewpoints: Approaches to defining and investigating fear. Nature Neuroscience. 2019;**22**(8):1205-1216. DOI: 10.1038/s41593-019-0456-6

[3] Rogers RW. A protection motivation theory of fear appeals and attitude change1. The Journal of Psychology. 1975;**91**(1):93-114. DOI: 10.1080/00223980.1975.9915803

[4] Kish-Gephart JJ, Detert JR, Treviño LK, Edmondson AC. Silenced by fear: The nature, sources, and consequences of fear at work. Research in Organizational Behavior. 2009;**29**:163-193. DOI: 10.1016/j.riob.2009.07.002

[5] Gibaldi C, Cusack G. Fear in the workplace. Review of Business. 2019;**39**:60-74

[6] Ashforth BE, Lee RT. Defensive behavior in organizations: A preliminary model. Human Relations. 1990;**43**(7):621-648. DOI: 10.1177/001872679004300702

[7] Northwestern Medicine. 5 Things You Never Knew about Fear. 2020 . Available from: https://www.nm.org/healthbeat/healthy-tips/emotional-health/5-things-you-never-knew-about-fear#:~:text=Fear%20Is%20Physical&text=Stress%20hormones%20like%20cortisol%20and,or%20run%20for%20your%20life. [Accessed: November 15, 2022]

[8] ComPsych. More than One-third of Employees Say "People Issues" Cause the Most Stress at Work. 2019 . Available from: https://www.compsych.com/press-room/press-article?nodeId=5e35641b-dfe3-4e87-9066-66c420b0a234. [Accessed: December 23, 2022]

[9] Lazarus RS. Why we should think of stress as a subset of emotion. In: Goldberger L, Breznitz S, editors. Handbook of Stress: Theoretical and Clinical Aspects. 2nd ed. New York, NY, USA: Free Press; 1993

[10] O'Donovan T. Competition and cooperation at work: The choices before us. The Way. 1994;**34**(2):106-115

[11] Brouwer R. When competition is the loser: The indirect effect of intra-team competition on team performance through task complexity, team conflict and psychological safety. In: 2016 49th Hawaii International Conference on System Sciences (HICSS). Koloa, HI, USA; 2016. pp. 1348-1357. DOI: 10.1109/HICSS.2016.170

[12] Wisse B, Rus D, Keller AC, Sleebos E. "Fear of losing power corrupts those who wield it": The combined effects of leader fear of losing power and competitive climate on leader self-serving behavior. European Journal of Work and Organizational Psychology. 2019;**28**(6):742-755. DOI: 10.1080/1359432X.2019.1635584

[13] Mangiapanello K, Hemmes N. An analysis of feedback from a behavior analytic perspective. Behavior Analyst. 2015;**38**(1):51-75. DOI: 10.1007/s40614-014-0026-x

[14] Peterson N. Fear is not a new principle of behavior. The Behavior Analyst. 1982;**5**:101-102. DOI: 10.1007/BF03393144

[15] VanStelle S, Vicars S, Harr V, Miguel C, Koerber J, Kazbour R, et al.

An objective review and analysis: 1998-2009. Journal of Organizational Behavior Management. 2012;**32**:93-123. DOI: 10.1080/01608061.2012.675864

[16] Johnson D, Johnson M, Dave P. Performance feedback in organizations: Understanding the functions, forms, and important features. Journal of Organizational Behavior Management. 2022;**2022**:1-26. DOI: 10.1080/01608061.2022.2089436

[17] O'Reilly CA III, Anderson JC. Trust and the communication of performance appraisal information: The effect of feedback on performance and job satisfaction. Human Communication Research. 1980;**6**(4):290-298. DOI: 10.1111/j.1468-2958.1980.tb00150.x

[18] Jawahar IM. An investigation of potential consequences of satisfaction with appraisal feedback. Journal of Leadership and Organizational Studies. 2006;**13**(2):14-28. DOI: 10.1177/1071791907013002010

[19] Simonian MJ, Brand D. Assessing the efficacy of and preference for positive and corrective feedback. Journal of Applied Behavior Analysis. 2022;**55**(3):727-745. DOI: 10.1002/jaba.911

[20] Jackman JM, Strober M. Fear of feedback. Harvard Business Review. 2003;**2003**:101-108

[21] DeNisi AS, Pritchard RD. Performance appraisal, performance management and improving individual performance: A motivational framework. Management and Organization Review. 2006;**2**(2):253-277. DOI: 10.1111/j.1740-8784.2006.00042.x

[22] Kang K, Oah S, Dickinson AM. The relative effects of different frequencies of feedback on work performance: A simulation. Journal of Organizational Behavior Management. 2005;**23**(4):21-53. DOI: 10.1300/J075v23n04_02

[23] Pampino RN Jr, MacDonald JE, Mullin JE, Wilder DA. Weekly feedback vs. daily feedback: An application in retail. Journal of Organizational Behavior Management. 2004;**23**(2-3):21-43. DOI: 10.1300/J075v23n02_03

[24] So Y, Lee K, Oah S. Relative effects of daily feedback and weekly feedback on customer service behavior at a gas station. Journal of Organizational Behavior Management. 2013;**33**(2):137-151. DOI: 10.1080/01608061,2013.785898

[25] Bell CM, Goldman A, Vogus C, Zhang I, Merritt S. Don't shoot the messenger: Causes and levers of manager performance appraisal anxiety. Journal of Organizational Psychology. 2020;**20**(6):83-99

[26] Gbadamosi G, Ross C. Perceived stress and performance appraisal discomfort: The moderating effects of core self-evaluations and gender. Public Personnel Management. 2012;**41**:637-659. DOI: 10.1177/00910261204100404

[27] Ferris GR, Munyon TP, Basik K, Buckley MR. The performance evaluation context: Social, emotional, cognitive, political, and relationship components. Human Resource Management Review. 2008;**18**(3):146-163. DOI: 10.1016/j.hrmr.2008.07.006

[28] Cawley BD, Keeping LM, Levy PE. Participation in the performance appraisal process and employee reactions: A meta-analytic review of field investigations. The Journal of Applied Psychology. 1998;**83**(4):615. DOI: 10.1037/0021-9010.83.4.615

[29] Peterson RS, Behfar KJ. The dynamic relationship between performance

feedback, trust, and conflict in groups: A longitudinal study. Organizational Behavior and Human Decision Processes. 2003;**92**(1-2):102-112. DOI: 10.1016/S0749-5978(03)00090-6

[30] Simons TL, Peterson RS. Task conflict and relationship conflict in top management teams: The pivotal role of intragroup trust. The Journal of Applied Psychology. 2000;**85**(1):102. DOI: 10.1037/0021-9010.85.1.102

[31] Mayer RC, Gavin MB. Trust in management and performance: Who minds the shop while the employees watch the boss? Academy of Management Journal. 2005;**48**(5):874-888. DOI: 10.5465/amj.2005.18803928

[32] Russell MB, Liggans GL. Fired up!: A guide to transforming your team from burnout to engagement. de Gruyter. 2022;**2022**:154. DOI: 10.1515/9783110741728

[33] Edmondson A. Psychological safety and learning behavior in work teams. Administrative Science Quarterly. 1999;**44**:350-383. DOI: 10.2307/266699

[34] Duhigg C. What Google learned from its quest to build the perfect team. The New York Times Magazine. 2016 . Available from: https://www.nytimes.com/2016/02/28/magazine/what-google-learned-from-its-quest-to-build-the-perfect-team.html?smid=pl-share. [Accessed: December 20, 2022]

[35] Google. Guide: Understand team Effectiveness. Re:Work . Available from: https://rework.withgoogle.com/print/guides/5721312655835136/. [Accessed: November 10, 2022]

[36] Rozovsky J. The Five Keys to a Successful Google Team. Re:Work. 2015 . Available from: https://rework.withgoogle.com/blog/five-keys-to-a-successful-google-team/. [Accessed: October 31, 2022]

[37] Edmondson, AC. The Fearless Organization: Creating Psychological Safety in the Workplace for Learning, Innovation, and Growth. Hoboken, NJ, USA: Wiley; 2018. Available from: https://learning.oreilly.com/library/view/the-fearless-organization/9781119477242/c01.xhtml. [Accessed: November 13, 2022]

[38] Forbes. Profile: Volkswagen Group . Available from: https://www.forbes.com/companies/volkswagen-group/?sh=79b98ef3130a. [Accessed: November 14, 2022]

[39] Hotten R. Volkswagen: The Scandal Explained. BBC News. 2015 . Available from: https://www.bbc.com/news/business-34324772. [Accessed: November 14, 2022]

[40] Parloff R. How VW paid $25 Billion Dollars for Dieselgate—and Got Off Easy. ProPublica. 2018. Available from: https://www.propublica.org/article/how-vw-paid-25-billion-for-dieselgate-and-got-off-easy. [Accessed: November 14, 2022]

[41] Cremer A, Bergin T. Fear and Respect – Volkswagen's Culture under Winterkorn. Reuters. 2015 . Available from: https://www.reuters.com/article/uk-volkswagen-emissions-culture/fear-and-respect-volkswagens-culture-under-winterkorn-idUKKCN0S40MN20151010. [Accessed: November 14, 2022]

[42] Ewing J, Bowley G. The Engineering of Volkswagen's Aggressive Ambition. The New York Times. 2015 . Available from: https://www.nytimes.com/2015/12/14/business/the-engineering-of-volkswagens-aggressiveambition.html. [Accessed: November 14, 2022]

[43] Sun M, Hagel J. Volkswagen tries to change workplace culture that fueled emissions scandal. Wall Street Journal. 2020 . Available from: https://www.wsj.com/articles/volkswagen-tries-to-change-workplace-culture-that-fueled-emissions-scandal-11601425486?reflink=desktopwebshare_permalink. [Accessed: November 14, 2022]

[44] Volkswagen. The foundation of the group's values . Available from https://www.volkswagenag.com/en/group/volkswagen-group-essentials.html. [Accessed: November 14, 2022]

[45] Whitten S. Bob Iger says Pixar was 'probably the best' acquisition he made during his tenure with Disney. CNBC. 2021 . Available from: https://www.cnbc.com/2021/12/21/disneys-bob-iger-says-pixar-was-probably-the-best-acquisition-as-ceo.html. [Accessed: December 16, 2022]

[46] Catmull E, Wallace A. Creativity, Inc: Overcoming the Unseen Forces that Stand in the Way of True Inspiration. New York, NY, USA: Random House; 2014. p. 480

[47] Catmull E. Inside the brain trust. Fast Company. 2014 . Available from: https://www.fastcompany.com/3027135/inside-the-pixar-braintrust. [Accessed: November 14, 2022]

Chapter 6

Perspective Chapter: We expect Effective Leadership from Leaders, but is this the Case in Reality? Reframing a Much-Hyped Phenomenon by Investigating the Antithesis

Tom Karp

Abstract

Leaders too often cause problems that challenge the effectivity of society and organisations; they exhibit bad leadership. This is an under-communicated and under-researched challenge, which is therefore investigated in the antithesis: What if leaders do not execute the effective leadership we expect of them, but quite the opposite, create problems and in-effectivity in the organisations they should serve? This is a more common challenge than many assume. Leadership is an inflated phenomenon that has somewhat distanced itself from organisational realities. There is, therefore, every reason to downscale the expectations of what can be achieved by leaders. This contribution is a nuanced analysis of leaders and their exercise of leadership. A powerful leadership industry has its own interests in promoting only the positive effects of leadership, with little interest in addressing human fallibility within the field. Other perspectives and research methods are therefore needed to avoid losing credibility and legitimacy as a research field and a resource base for professional practice. Given the human and financial toll that fallible leaders take, the advice for organisations and institutions is to develop better policies, systems, and processes that weed out negative and destructive behaviour.

Keywords: leadership, leaders, antithesis, destructive, negative, ineffective, inflated, reality

1. Introduction

The aim of leadership should be to work towards solutions and the greater good, and bring about progress and development for nations, institutions, organisations, and individuals. According to Yukl, 'Effective leadership at all levels of society and in all our organisations is essential for coping with the growing social, economic, and environmental problems confronting the world. Learning to cope with these problems is not a luxury but a necessity' ([1], p. 422). This premise, which has support among many scholars [2–6] and practitioners, implies that leadership is important. Day further [7] claimed that leadership explains more than 40 percent of the variance in organisational performance [8]. Avolio and colleagues argued that leadership interventions produced a 66 percent probability of achieving a positive outcome [9]. Others [10] have referred to evolutionary psychology as well as historical leaders and achievements in China, the Roman Empire, the Church, and military organisations in seeking to prove that leadership matters, as they assert that humans are biologically and psychologically conditioned for leadership and followership [11].

There is a tendency to attribute outcomes to people in salient positions [12]. An over-optimistic belief in leadership is also due to reverse attribution, wherein people seek to identify a leader thought to have caused success, even when arguments suggest otherwise. This has resulted in the construction of a seductive and overly positive research field and practice. This construction is supported by easy-to-sell concepts, tools, motivating TED-like talks, and a huge volume of best-selling books providing recipes for success. All are based on the thesis that leaders are important, and their exercise of leadership contributes to progress for nations, organisations, and individuals.

This may be the case, but to challenge a powerful stance, the antithesis is examined herein: What if leadership—and leaders—rather than helping to find solutions and provide progress, are sometimes the source of problems, inefficiency, and destructiveness? Numerous corporate scandals involving lying, cheating, larceny, and greed point to failure among leaders and justify such enquiry, as do reports of corporate lapses and catastrophes that conclude that the problems could be traced back to failures in leadership and a lack of appropriate leadership quality. Therefore, there are justified qualms about the quality of leaders and their exercise of leadership [13]. Within leadership studies, such perspectives are referred to as the dark side of leadership. The underlying assumption among many, however, is that the negative effects of leadership are an anomaly. It is striking how little leadership research has focused on the negative effects of leadership [14]. Scholars have been more concerned with studying leadership behaviours that should be encouraged than with researching negative, even unhealthy, aspects of leadership.

One could therefore argue that the field of leadership needs to be protected from itself and steadily increasing self-confidence, which is not always justified. The current scholarly leadership field exaggerates what can be achieved through leadership and downplays its negative aspects. Consequently, a more sober analysis of leadership and its contribution to society and organisations is needed. In this respect, business schools play an important role in challenging the leadership industry, which has a vested interest in hyping leadership. Further, researchers need a greater focus on realities rather than ideals, as we need to know more about leadership in complex, lived, everyday organisational realities. The study of leadership should also take a greater interest in human fallibility and discuss the under-researched and under-communicated darker sides of leadership.

This chapter is conceptual and draws on literature from critical theory and studies of managerial work and leadership practice. It is structured as follows: First, the worrying signals that suggest that there are frequent problems with the exercise of leadership are discussed. Second, examples of the problem-creating behaviour of leaders, a behaviour more common than one should think, are elaborated. Third, corrective measures are suggested. Lastly, the chapter concludes with the contention that the antithesis discussed herein needs to be taken more seriously if the leadership field is to advance and contribute solutions and progress to societal and organisational challenges.

2. Unhealthy and unproductive work environments

Studies on performance indicate that many leaders are ineffective, incompetent, or even complete failures [15–17]. They may bully and abuse power, acts that are potentially damaging to employees' health [18]. Bullying from leaders is the greatest source of unhappiness among employees and leads to higher rates of sickness leave and resignation [19]. A Norwegian study suggests that up to 3 percent of employees report they are bullied by people in leadership roles at work [20]. Further, approximately 25 percent of employees stated that their effectiveness at work was impaired due to bullying by leaders. According to approximately 20 percent of respondents, this bullying reduced their job satisfaction [14]. It is difficult to assess whether such figures are generally representative, but there is reason to think that they are. Evidently, situational factors obviously influence such an analysis. It is a leader's role to exert influence and authority, but finding socially acceptable ways of exerting authority while exercising consistent leadership seems to be difficult in many cultures [21]. Moreover, it is well documented that power corrupts [22–24].

There is also evidence that only 30 percent of organisations experience a healthy work environment [25, 26]. Employee satisfaction surveys indicate that dealing with one's immediate superior is the most stressful part of one's job [27, 28]. Most important to work itself and closely linked to leaders' actions—or lack thereof—are control and autonomy over one's own job, given leaders' micromanagement and excessive control. A lack of job control affects mental health and physical health outcomes. For a subordinate, not being able to influence one's own work environment is stressful and a source of powerlessness, regardless of the jobholder's salary or formal status [29–31]. Therefore, job autonomy is one of the most important predictors of job satisfaction and work motivation and is frequently ranked higher even than pay [32].

The consequences of the above shortcomings have a negative influence on subordinates' working attitudes [33] and lead to increased depression, stress, insecurity, and fear [34]; decreased task performance, satisfaction, and well-being [35]; poorer leader–subordinate relationships [36]; increased work conflict [37] and turnover [33]; and decreased organisational commitment [38]. Contextual and situational factors obviously affect the behaviour of both leaders and subordinates. Consequently, the antithesis is not only due to the leaders themselves. Evidently, contextual, and situational factors also trigger destructive behaviour in both leaders and subordinates, and place constraints on what leaders can achieve; however, this is a question of degree and frequency. Achieving operational excellence is a massive challenge for most organisations [39] and is even more challenging when leadership is ineffective.

3. Constraints to effective leadership

Unhealthy and unproductive work environments are often due to a lack of high-quality leadership raw material—the people who are attracted by and recruited to leadership positions. There is a relationship between a desire for power and advancement to leadership positions [40, 41]. However, here we find a double-edged sword.

Some of the forces driving leaders to seek power may also be destructive [42]. Qualities that may be important for leaders also contain elements of psychoticism [43]. This includes traits such as aggression, egocentrism, and narcissism [44]—even sadistic traits [45]. Personality research indicates that narcissism, paranoia, and character deviation influence how leadership is played out [46], and a 'dark triad' personality refers to the toxic cocktail of narcissism, Machiavellianism, and psychopathy [47]. These qualities can propel leaders forward, but they may also be associated with personality disorders and ineffective leadership.

The aforementioned traits, individually and collectively, produce dysfunctional leaders who may act destructively and tyrannically and are likely to engage in micromanagement. Leadership positions thus seem to appeal to individuals with self-centred, status-obsessed, emotionally cold, and aggressive personalities. Dysfunctional personality types are disproportionately represented in executive positions [48], as these positions offer large opportunities for personal gain and privileges, while the risks of loss are correspondingly small.

People not suited for leadership should obviously not be recruited to positions of power, but search and selection processes may be flawed. A lack of competence among recruiters is one reason for this [49]. Findings also indicate that candidates who are extroverted and confident are more often recruited than those who are humble, introverted, and realistic about the challenges of a leadership job [50]. It is thus a paradox that when organisations are recruiting leaders, they often want individuals who are energetic and able to accomplish a lot, can make tough decisions, possess self-confidence, and be strong [44]. Paradoxically, these are the same characteristics found in people with a high degree of narcissistic traits [51].

However, as many leaders learn to hide such traits, they remain undetected by the people who employ them [52], as many recruitment and selection processes overly focus on the positive aspects of leadership. In general, organisations seem to have great self-confidence in their ability to find the right leadership candidates. However, this self-confidence is not always justified [53]. Search and selection processes strive to predict the future performance of leaders, and it is estimated by some scholars that leaders are mis-employed in as much as 50 percent of cases [54, 55]. Mathematicians' simulations even suggest that the base rate of leader incompetence is between 50 and 75 percent, leading researchers to suggest that organisations sometimes would be better off choosing leaders by pulling names from a hat than from an evaluation process [56].

There are constraints to effective leadership in most organisations [50, 57, 58]. Leaders work under difficult framework conditions. They often must function in unclear roles and survive hectic workdays with cross-pressures, resource scarcity, target conflicts, stress, and friction. Leaders at the lower, middle, and top levels in both the private and public sectors often face high performance pressures, hectic and long workdays, time pressure, uncertainty, pressure to constantly change, restructuring requirements, emotionally charged situations that they must deal with, and difficulties that they must resolve. They also need to manage scarce resources and tight budgets. They often have many stakeholders to attend to and may experience conflicts between goals and means. They need to balance stability with change, short-term goals with long-term visions, and organisational development while launching new strategic initiatives. Therefore, few leaders have the knowledge, skills, and abilities needed to cope with such a wide range of tasks and challenges, and most work against the odds [59].

Thus, we ought to lower expectations and not always expect effective leadership from leaders; instead, we should, as a minimum, expect leaders not to create problems and ineffectiveness in organisations by abusing power, bullying, creating unhealthy work environments, or otherwise exhibiting destructive behaviour. If it is the case that ineffective behaviour from leaders is taking place more often than expected, the more interesting enquiry, then, is why does the leadership community still cling to the thesis that leadership is effective, important, and positive, and under-research and under-communicate the antithesis?

4. A powerful leadership industry that clings to the ideals

Not surprisingly, there are stakeholders with a vested interest in keeping alive the thesis that leadership is important while inflating the importance of leaders. This applies to the leaders themselves, as well as to the boards on which they sit, leadership developers, management consultants, head-hunters, leadership researchers, and business schools. There is a powerful leadership industry sweet-talking leadership, which makes a living claiming that leadership is important [60, 61]. During the last 30 years or so, a 'global theory industry' has emerged with powerful players [62]. The players are reputable business schools and large international consulting companies. They partly live off developing and selling new theories, solutions, methods, and tools to leaders. Further, they inflate the importance of leaders leading and the importance of organisations selecting the right leaders, as well as paying them well.

In academia, the focus on leadership is relatively new. The 1990s saw increased attention to leadership, whereas before then, organisations were administered or managed [13]. Over the last 30 years, the number of scientific articles on leadership in international journals has exploded. Leadership research is often normative; that is, it focuses on what leaders should do but says less about what they actually do—the mundane, everyday activities leaders often spend most of their time on. This is perhaps due to a need to justify the field of study and gain academic recognition, as well as to the implicit assumption that leadership is regarded as important. It may also be due to tactical reasons for ambitious researchers to publish articles that support normative models and the theses related to these models. Leadership is thus an intellectually weak field due to ideological undertones and methodological reductionism [57]. The field struggles to gain academic recognition. There is little agreement about theoretical frameworks in the field; there are no generally accepted universal theories that can be tested, and methodologies and analytical techniques are not always sufficiently rigorous. Further, the large number of leadership gurus, superficial concepts, and airport bestseller-style publications do little to enhance the seriousness of the field.

In much of the leadership literature, in MBA courses, and in leadership development programmes, leadership is commonly presented as an ordered and controllable activity, but such assumptions are of limited use in real-life situations, where leaders must cope with many demands, as well as complexity, and uncertainty. Leaders commonly operate in stressful environments with conflicting expectations, and their work is more likely to be characterised by reacting to events, fragmentation, and a hectic pace than by order [63]. Thus, there is a gap between the normative ideals presented in the leadership literature and the reality faced by many leaders. People, however, seem to want the ideals; they want their leaders to be good people who work for the common good. Fairhurst and Connaughton exemplified this misconception by arguing that 'leadership actors are reflexive practitioners who shape and are shaped by realities they co-create. They also have the capacity for morally grounded, relationally responsive action as they account for their actions to themselves and others' [64].

One may argue that leadership is ultimately a moral endeavour [65], especially as the activity involves the use of power, to which one needs bulwarks in the form of moral and ethical reflection. Belonging to a species whose members justify their actions morally, people, including leaders, commonly think of themselves as good and their behaviour as defensible, even when these propositions are objectively dubious [66]. Consequently, in much of the literature, the authors frame leadership as something good or, at least, effective. Thus, leadership is used, at least subconsciously, as a 'hallelujah' word. Leaders do good things, many seem to assume. They help people and organisations develop. In the leadership literature, we will therefore not read so much about leaders doing bad leadership [67].

The bulk of the leadership literature, therefore, provides an abundance of success stories about business leaders, tech entrepreneurs, and political leaders. It would be fine if such an understanding of leadership reflects reality, but often it does not. First, other perspectives on leadership fade into the background, crowded out by the volume of feel-good literature, TED-like talks, and glossy leadership concepts. Second, the understanding that leadership is always effective is self-reinforcing and leads many to look for facts that confirm preconceived assumptions. Third, the search for efficient leadership creates unrealistic expectations of what leaders can achieve. Lastly, there are leaders, as argued herein, who do not practice effective leadership; thus, we cannot say that leadership is always effective. Since leaders have the power and opportunities to make a difference in people's lives, we certainly want them to be people with good qualities, and this leads to attribution. Many, therefore, cling to the hope that leaders are good people who want to achieve the best for the community or society. People need the illusion, but the wish to identify goodness in leadership sometimes clouds reality.

5. A failure to address human fallibility

Leaders, like most others, are fallible; they are not always perfect, good, effective, and able to work for the greater good. Steinbeck, the Nobel Prize-winning author, wrote that human societies tend to share universal descriptions of good and bad human qualities, yet in some societal contexts, the people who possess those so-called 'bad' qualities are successful, while those who possess the 'good' qualities fail [68, p. 80]. The author further writes, 'perhaps no other animal is so torn between alternatives. Man might be described fairly adequately, if simply, as a two-legged paradox' [68, p. 80].

Errare humanum est, one says in Latin, 'to err is human'. This applies to leaders, but in the literature, the focus is rarely on 'to err' and not always even on 'human' but on superhuman strengths and potential. One may find support in the tendency of human societies and their institutions to fragment into a Hobbesian view of society with competing groups, leaving people all too ready to adopt prejudices and pursue quarrels, disputes, and even feuds [69]. Human beings have the intellectual and cultural capacity to form functioning societies, institutions, and organisations, but they frequently fail to use this capacity properly. The result is societies torn apart by war, violence, crime, dissension, and inequality, and organisations ruined by destructiveness, power struggles, inefficiency, miscommunication, and disorder. Scholars struggle to understand why this is the case, variously appointing blame to nature, nurture, government, politics, leaders, short-sightedness, greed, and selfishness. Human beings obviously have predispositions to cooperate, to discriminate between the trustworthy and the treacherous, to be trustworthy, to earn good reputations, to exchange goods and information, and to organise work that needs to be done [70]. The human mind also has the ability to build social cooperation and create positive human interactions. In fact, cooperativeness may be said to be the very hallmark of being human and what sets us apart from other species [71]. Obviously, most leaders have the intellect, instincts, and temperament to foster the greater good, progress, and effective work environments, whereas others foster self-interest, conflict, and antisocial behaviour. Therefore, most leaders—as well as their subordinates—are far more nuanced than they appear in the bulk of the leadership literature.

One can obviously choose to disregard leadership as a discipline altogether and instead study and practice administrative behaviour. Disregard the last 30 years of leadership hype. According to Kellerman ([60], p. 200), 'Leadership is in danger of becoming obsolete' [72]. If leaders and their poor performance of leadership are the source of problems, not the providers of solutions, the remedy may be to eliminate the leader profession altogether and organise alternative decision-making and coordination mechanisms, such as self-governing groups, autonomous organisations, and shared or distributed leadership. However, this is easier said than done. Leadership is strongly tied to our cultural web and is connected to human psychology and biology. There will always be leaders. It is therefore valid to maintain an interest in leadership and leaders, as they often have an impact, one way or the other, on other people's lives.

6. Challenging the dominating positive leadership narrative

Hegelian dialectic comprises the thesis, the antithesis, and the tension between the two being resolved by means of synthesis [73]. The thesis within most leadership research and practice is that leaders are instrumental for ensuring progress in organisations, institutions, and societies. There is obvious support for such a claim, although the evidence is not as solid as many have argued. The antithesis is that leaders do not always provide progress; on the contrary, they create problems, destructiveness, and in-effectivity in organisations and societies. Obviously, one may argue that studies indicating such behaviour are merely anecdotal rather than representative evidence, but this is not a productive way forward. Instead, we should challenge the dominating narrative told and sold by the leadership community.

One obvious solution is to promote critical thinking. Reading critical theory would, of course, not guarantee that leaders behave better, but critical perspectives are potentially far-reaching in the study and practice of leadership [74]. Critical thinking raises several relevant leadership issues in contemporary organisations and societies. Examples are power/identity dialectics, elite problems, simplistic notions of 'leader' and 'follower', and differences and inequalities in organisations in the form of gender, ethnicity, class, age, disability, faith, and national origin. Critical perspectives also challenge an important premise: that leadership is associated with membership in an elite, handpicked group of people who share specific attributes that they can learn/develop and thereby are destined to govern others. This idea is particularly rooted in the grooming place for most leaders, the leadership education and development community.

Business schools are important players in the production of leadership research and theory, beyond being the source of education preferred by many leaders. The doorway to knowledge matters. Business schools have received much criticism in recent years. In particular, there is a call for many schools to better connect themselves to the realities of the organisational world and resist the urge to invent an abstract world that they find more attractive—a temptation that goes back to the ancient interplay of Platonic and Aristotelian approaches to the world. This is for reasons that are methodical, as well as financial and strategic. The elephant in the room in this discussion is financial; there is less money to be made on teaching the antithesis than on marketing, educating, and researching the positive effects of leadership. In 2011, the American Association of Business estimated that there were around 13,000 business schools in the world employing huge numbers of people and graduating large volumes of students leaving campuses with business, management, or leadership-related degrees. In 2013, the top 20 US MBA programmes charged at least 100,000 USD. Parker (2018) thus estimated that business schools globally have an income of at least 400 billion USD [75]. We can further add the market for accreditation agencies, textbooks, scientific journals, and conferences. In 1970, Illich argued that business schools have become places that hoard knowledge and then distribute it to reward those who can pay and conform to certain expectations [76].

The radical solution is to dismantle the business schools in their present forms altogether and reimagine schooling as a web of communication, cooperation, and peer-to-peer learning, without the professors, certificates, and degrees. Technology development already assists in such a shift, as more and more courses are distributed online and made cheaper and even free of charge. Schools are, therefore, already shifting their strategic focus to adapt to this change. However, business schools will, of course, not let go of their revenues or their monopoly on research-based knowledge. Given that most schools are pragmatic institutions and instrumental in their decision-making, if sources of funding from central government bodies, supranational institutions, and research bodies are directed towards business schools to provide more nuanced perspectives, the schools will realign their strategies.

Further, much research has been pursuing the wrong kind of relevance: primarily relevance to business organisations and their effectiveness rather than relevance to the complex problems that matter to society and work environments. Why study leadership at all if the objective is simply to predict business effectiveness? All that time and money spent on studying and practicing leadership is for nothing if leadership does not have a positive impact on people, organisations, and society. Revised research strategies and directions therefore need to include fresh thinking about the value of leadership and leaders. This applies to problems that stimulate better methods for selecting the most suited to lead, better transparency in organisations, and improved measures and standards for work force productivity, well-being, and health.

7. Addressing messy organisational realities

Much leadership research, teaching, and development has de-coupled itself from organisational realities. Consider the following statement from Burns:

> *I believe leadership is not only a descriptive term but a prescriptive one, embracing a moral, even a passionate, dimension. Consider our common usage. We do not call for good leadership—we expect, or at least hope, that it will be good. 'Bad' leadership implies no leadership. I contend there is nothing neutral about leadership; it is valued as a moral necessity ([77], p. 2).*

By stating this, Burns disregarded many leaders from the leadership profession, as many of them do not embrace morality or passion or perform what he calls 'good leadership'. He falls into the same trap as many others. They idealise leaders because they need to believe in something bigger than themselves. When somebody is given power and the right to govern others, people would like that person to be a person who adheres to ideals and morals and uses the given power wisely, fairly, and justly.

Two decades ago, Starkey and Madan sparked a debate over whether the predominance of an overly academic and theoretical mode of knowledge production has given rise to a relevance gap between research and the organisations that such research should serve, and ultimately whether leadership research is reproducing itself [78]. A large volume of leadership studies is based on quantitative analyses using questionnaires in which a limited number of variables are examined, leading to reductionism and simplistic casual explanations that are often distant from organisational reality. When Lowe and Gardner summarised the research methods used in empirical articles in the first 10 years of the journal *The Leadership Quarterly*, they found that 64 percent of them used a questionnaire-based approach [79]. A later analysis of the second 10 years confirmed the same trend [80]. Kaiser et al. concluded that most leadership research concerns how individual leaders are perceived and provides less data about the actual process of leadership [81]. Researchers have, to a great extent, researched a population—leaders—that is tangible and easy to measure. There has been less research on the phenomenon—leadership—the processes, interactions, relationships, subordinates, and contextual and structural frameworks.

The remedies would, of course, complicate the work of researchers and obstruct the measurement, number crunching, and easy routes to being published. Studies of leadership should, at a minimum, be supplemented with methods that move out of the idealised world and study actual work practices, not loosely or disconnected representations. Research needs to refrain from dichotomies and tautologies and avoid packaging what may be a scattered and ambiguous set of behaviours and responses into a categorised leadership concept. A more nuanced view of the role of leadership and the work of leaders would not lessen their significance. Leadership often matters, for good or for bad.

There is therefore a need to connect with the messy, complex, volatile, and uncertain reality experienced in organisations, not some constructed hyper-reality modelled in questionnaires or interviews with leaders themselves, in which they inflate their doings. Bryman noted that little has changed since Conger's call for greater use of participant observation in the study of leadership, acknowledging that leadership studies are over-reliant on questionnaires [82, 83]. Since leadership studies overwhelmingly focus on behaviour, the infrequent use of observation of interaction and lived experience is surprising. Such research would reveal the messy reality in which most leaders and subordinates operate and the gap between the idealised models and the everyday complexity they experience [84]. Moving leadership research forward will also require multidisciplinary and interdisciplinary efforts, as well as time-consuming in-depth studies. This explains why some researchers are reluctant to study leadership embedded in organisational reality, along with the fact that such data offer fewer opportunities for quantitative analysis that give their studies more 'scientific' packaging. As a research community, we know enough about the ideals; we need to know more about lived organisational realities and actual practices of leadership.

8. Darker sides of leadership complement the understanding

Bad leadership is not leadership, claimed Burns above [77], but this is not a sound argument. Bad leadership, in its many shades of grey or even black, is not uncommon, and it needs to be studied and understood. Specific research strands have addressed destructiveness [85–88], toxic leadership [89–92], and the darker side of leadership in general [83, 93, 94]. Terms such as negative leadership [95], narcissistic leadership [96], abusive leadership [97], tyrannical leadership [33], derailed leadership [98], and unethical leadership [99] are also in use, spotlighting a lack of competence, character, and/or care by the leader. The common factor of such studies is that people in organisations, including the leaders themselves, are not just conscious, highly focused, rational individuals. They are also subject to (often contractionary) wishes, desires, conflicts, defensive behaviours, and anxieties—some conscious, others beyond consciousness—but this is not a much-taken perspective within leadership studies. Even the most successful organisational leaders are prone to irrational behaviour, an anomaly often ignored by researchers.

Much of what goes on between people in organisations takes place in the intrapsychic and interpersonal worlds of organisational members [100]. The underlying mental activity and behaviour are therefore of interest, as well as the causes that influence human behaviour and the forces affecting people's behaviour, preventing them from being effective. If we are to understand why leaders do not always engage in effective leadership, then we must understand the conflicts, protection mechanisms, tensions, and feelings that affect leadership behaviour. Darker sides of human behaviour make leaders misperceive situations and conversations and act in inappropriate ways. Disciplines such as psychodynamics, psychoanalysis, psychotherapy, developmental psychology, and neuropsychology contribute to an understanding of the above [101–103]. The premise is that a portion of the regulation of people's behaviour takes place outside the domain of conscious awareness. This gives rise to defensive reactions, innate response patterns, and scripts that in many cases have outlived their effectiveness. The result may be that people use different types of destructive behaviour in their interaction with others [104].

The above themes are under-researched and under-communicated in leadership studies. More research into the darker sides of leadership has the potential to provide a more comprehensive perspective of leadership, giving recruiters and organisations better support on how to deal with such issues. Research on the darker sides of leadership has made much progress over the last two decades, but it is still a young field. Research is needed on more than destructive traits; we also need to study actual leader behaviour, rather than only follower perceptions, as well as contextual variables [105].

9. Conclusion

The field of leadership is inflated because of the somewhat infinite belief in the essentiality of leadership, while it is also the case that leaders cause problems and ineffectiveness. It may even appear that the darker, or at least grey, sides of leadership are often the norm, rather than the exception, in numerous organisations, institutions, and societies. This is obviously troubling, both because of the challenges this creates and the formation of a scholarly field that has somewhat distanced itself from the reality that the field was intended to address. This mismatch has been under-researched and under-communicated.

Of course, there are many leaders who do a good, even excellent, job, but it is difficult to assess the representativity of such people, given that research is overly focused on the positive effects of leadership and neglects its negative aspects. This is because there is a powerful leadership industry that has its own interests in promoting positive leadership as well as the need to scientifically justify a growing and important field of study. There is also little interest in addressing human fallibility within leadership studies, overshadowed by the assumption that leaders are good people without too many faults. Corrective actions are needed in this respect to avoid the loss of credibility and legitimacy as a research field and as a resource base for professional leadership practice. Otherwise, we will continue to nurture an elitist field of study that lacks focus on what is really occurring in organisations, along with the influence of gender, culture, religion, and demographics, and the organisational, structural, and contextual realities. This will neither serve society as a whole nor the field as a research discipline or as a resource base for leaders.

The theoretical contribution herein is a nuanced analysis of leadership. Problem-creating behaviour and destructiveness by leaders are more common than many assume. The present chapter also contributes to the debate about which research methods are best suited for studying leadership. Studying complex, lived organisational realities is best achieved by an increased use of research methods such as ethnography, autoethnography, discourse analysis, action research and multi-method approaches. The challenge is that such methods, which may be demanding in terms of time and resources, are not always favoured by top journals, and are therefore easily down prioritised by researchers in pursuit of publications and citations.

For practitioners, given the human and financial toll that fallible leaders take, the advice for organisations and institutions is to develop better policies and systems that weed out those not suited for leadership. Further, they should instigate processes that institutionalise destructive-intolerant cultures, as well as increase the transparency and accountability of leadership to deal with, adjust for, and correct human fallibility. Accordingly, there is every reason to downscale the expectations of what leaders can achieve, at least within short timeframes, in organisations.

Author details

Tom Karp
Kristiania University College, Oslo, Norway

*Address all correspondence to: tom.karp@kristiania.no

References

[1] Yukl GA. Leadership in Organizations. 8th ed. Boston, Ma: Pearson; 2013

[2] Bass BM. The Bass Handbook of Leadership: Theory, Research, and Managerial Applications. 4th ed. New York: Free Press; 2008

[3] Bennis W. The challenges of leadership in the modern world: Introduction to the special issue. American Psychologist. 2007;**62**(1):2-5

[4] Day DV, Antonakis J. The Nature of Leadership. Thousand Oaks, Calif: Sage; 2012

[5] Drucker PF. Management: Tasks, Responsibilities, Practises. New York: Harper Business; 1973

[6] Western S. Leadership: A Critical Text. Thousand Oaks: Sage; 2008

[7] Day DV. Introduction: Leadership and organizations. In: Day D, editor. Oxford Handbook of Organization and Leadership. Oxford: Oxford University Press. pp. 3-21

[8] Day DV, Lord RG. Executive leadership and organizational performance: Suggestions for a new theory and methodology. Journal of Management. 1988;**14**(3):453-464

[9] Avolio BJ, Reichard RJ, Hannah ST, Walumbwa FO, Chan A. A meta-analytic review of leadership impact research: Experimental and quasi-experimental studies. The Leadership Quarterly. 2009;**20**(5):764-784

[10] Van Vugt M. Evolutionary Origins of Leadership and Followership. Personality and Social Psychology Review. 2006;**10**(4):354-371

[11] Burns JM. Leadership. New York: Harper & Row; 1978

[12] Meindl JR. The romance of leadership as a follower-centric theory: A social constructionist approach. The Leadership Quarterly. 1995;**6**(3):329-341

[13] Storey J, Hartley J, Denis JL, Ulrich D. Preface. In: Storey J, Hartley J, Denis JL, Ulrich D, editors. The Routledge Companion to Leadership. New York: Routledge; 2017

[14] Einarsen S, Raknes BI, Matthiesen SB, Hellesøy OH. Mobbing og personkonflikter. Helsefarlig samspill på arbeidsplassen. Nordisk Psykologi. Bergen: Sigma Forlag; 1994

[15] Burke RJ. Why leaders fail: Exploring the darkside. International Journal of Manpower. 2006;**27**(1):91-100

[16] Gentry B. Derailment: How successful leaders avoid it. In: The ASTD Leadership Handbook. Alexandria: STD Press; 2010

[17] Hogan R, Hogan J. Assessing Leadership: A View from the Dark Side. International Journal of Selection and Assessment. 2001;**9**(1&2):40-51

[18] Vartia M, Leka S. Interventions for the prevention and management of bullying at work. Bullying and Harassment in the Workplace: Developments in Theory, Research, and Practice. 2011;**2**:359-379

[19] Teglkamp S. Sygefravær: Skurken er ofte dårlig ledelse. København: Væksthus for ledelse [Internet]. 2018. Available from: https://www.lederweb.dk/artikler/sygefravaer-skurken-er-ofte-daarlig-ledelse/. [Accessed: 2020-12-10]

[20] Einarsen S, Skogstad A, Aasland MS, Løseth AMS. Destruktivt lederskap: Årsaker og konsekvenser. In: Skogstad A, Einarsen S, editors. Ledelse på godt og vondt. Bergen: Fagbokforlaget; 2002. pp. 233-254

[21] Hofstede G. Culture's Consequences. Beverly Hills: SAGE; 1980

[22] Fast NJ, Gruenfeld DH, Sivanathan N, Galinsky AD. Illusory control: A generative force behind power's far-reaching effects. Psychological Science. 2009;**20**(4):502-508

[23] Lai L. Makt og påvirkningskraft: Hvordan få gjennomslag på jobben. Oslo: Cappelen Damm Akademisk; 2014

[24] Lammers J, Galinsky AD, Gordijn EH, Otten S. Illegitimacy moderates the effects of power on approach. Psychological Science. 2008;**19**(6):558-564

[25] Mawritz MB, Mayer DM, Hoobler JM, Wayne SJ, Marinova SV. A trickle-down model of abusive supervision. Personnel Psychology. 2012;**65**(2):325-357

[26] Neilson GL, Pasternack BA, Van Nuys KE. The passive-aggressive organization. Harvard Business Review. 2005;**83**(10):82-92

[27] Hogan R. Personality and the Fate of Organizations. Hillsdale: Erlbaum; 2007

[28] Kaiser RB, Curphy G. Leadership development: The failure of an industry and the opportunity for consulting psychologists. Consulting Psychology Journal: Practice and Research. 2013;**65**(4):294-302

[29] Chandola T, Brunner E, Marmot M. Chronic stress at work and the metabolic syndrome: Prospective study. British Medical Journal. 2006;**332**(7540): 521-525

[30] Karasek R. Lower health risk with increased job control among white collar workers. Journal of Organizational Behavior. 1990;**11**(3):171-185

[31] Pisljar T, van der Lippe T, den Dulk L. Health among hospital employees in Europe: A cross-national study of the impact of work stress and work control. Social Science & Medicine. 2011;**72**(6):899-906

[32] Boffey PM. Satisfaction on the Job: Autonomy Ranks First. New York Times; 1985

[33] Tepper BJ, Henle CA, Lambert LS, Giacalone RA, Duffy MK. Abusive supervision and subordinates' organization deviance. Journal of Applied Psychology. 2008;**93**(4): 721-732

[34] Schat ACH, Frone MR. Exposure to psychological aggression at work and job performance: The mediating role of job attitudes and personal health. Work & Stress. 2011;**25**(1):23-40

[35] Tepper BJ. Abusive supervision in work organizations: Review, synthesis, and research agenda. Journal of Management. 2007;**33**(3):261-289

[36] Tepper BJ, Carr JC, Breaux DM, Geider S, Hu C, Hua W. Abusive supervision, intentions to quit, and employees' workplace deviance: A power/ dependence analysis. Organizational Behavior and Human Decision Processes. 2009;**109**(2):156-167

[37] Zellars KL, Tepper BJ, Duffy MK. Abusive supervision and subordinates' organizational citizenship behavior. Journal of Applied Psychology. 2002;**87**(6):1068-1076

[38] Ashforth BE. Petty Tyranny in organizations: A preliminary examination of antecedents and consequences. Canadian Journal of Administrative Sciences. 1997;**8**(14):126-140

[39] Sadun R, Bloom N, Van Reenen J. Why do we undervalue competent management? Harvard Business Review. 2017;**19**:120-127

[40] Howard A, Bray DW. Managerial Lives in Transition: Advancing Age and Changing Times. New York: Guilford Press; 1988

[41] McClelland DC, Boyatzis RE. Leadership motive pattern and long-term success in management. Journal of Applied Psychology. 1982;**67**(6):737-743

[42] Moe HT, Strand M, Karp T, Nordbom HM. Cortisol and testosterone in leadership practice. Psych. 2021;**3**(2):153-162

[43] Eysenck HJ. The Biological Basis of Personality. Piscataway, NJ: Transaction Publishers; 1967

[44] Martinsen ØL, Glasø L. Personlighet og ledelse. In: Glasø L, Matthiesen SB, editors. Livet som leder Lederundersøkelsen 30. Bergen: Fagbokforlaget; 2013. pp. 47-74

[45] Goethals GR, Allison ST. The Romance of Heroism and Heroic Leadership. Bingley, UK: Emerald; 2019

[46] Kernberg OF. Ideology, conflict, and leadership in groups and organizations. New Haven: Yale University Press; 1998

[47] Paulhus DL, Williams KM. The dark triad of personality: Narcissism, Machiavellianism, and psychopathy. Journal of Research in Personality. 2002;**36**(6):556-563

[48] Babiak P, Hare RD. Snakes in Suits. New York: Harper Collins; 2009

[49] Skorstad E. Rett person på rett plass. Oslo: Gyldendal akademisk; 2015

[50] Mintzberg H. Managing. Harlow: Pearson; 2009

[51] Brandebo MF, Alvinius A. Introductory chapter: Dark sides of organizations and leadership - An integrative approach and definitions. In: Brandebo MF, Alvinius A, editors. Dark Sides of Organizational Behavior and Leadership. London, United Kingdom: Intechopen; 2019

[52] Hjort K. En dårlig leder kan også være en god leder. In: Pissedårlig ledelse. von Oettingen A, Mellon K, edited by København: Hans Reitzels Forlag; 2020. pp. 34-42

[53] Schmidt FL, Hunter JE. The validity and utility of selection methods in personnel psychology: Practical and theoretical implications of 85 years of research findings. Psychological Bulletin. 1998;**124**(2):262

[54] Arnulf JK. Lederutvikling. In: Kuvaas B, editor. Evidens Basert HR. Oslo: Fagbokforlaget; 2008. pp. 200-215

[55] Lucier CP, Kocourek P, Habbel R. CEO Succession 2005: The Crest of the Wave [Internet. Strategy+Business; 2006. Available from: https://www.strategy-business.com/article/06210?gko=5183f Accessed: 2021-01-06

[56] Abrahams M. Random Promotion may be Best, Research Suggests [Internet]. The Guardian; 2010. Available from: https://www.theguardian.com/education/2010/nov/01/random-promotion-research [Accessed: 2020-12-10]

[57] Alvesson M. Waiting for Godot: Eight major problems in the odd field of leadership studies. Leadership. 2019;**15**(1):27-43

[58] Karp T. We are asking the wrong question about leadership: The case for 'good-enough'leadership. In: Dark Sides of Organizational Behavior and Leadership. London: IntechOpen; 2018

[59] Hogan R, Kaiser RB. What we know about leadership. Review of General Psychology. 2005;**9**(2):169-180

[60] Kellerman B. The End of Leadership. New York: Harper Business; 2012

[61] Pfeffer J. Leadership BS. New York: Harpercollins Publishers; 2015

[62] Micklethwait J, Wooldridge A. The Witch Doctors: What Management Gurus Are Saying, Why It Matters and How to Make Sense of It. New York: Times Books; 1996

[63] Tengblad S. The Work of Managers. Oxford: Oxford University Press; 2012

[64] Fairhurst GT, Connaughton SL. Leadership: A communicative perspective. Leadership. 2014;**10**(1):7-35

[65] Ciulla JB. Ethics: The Heart of Leadership. Westport: Praeger; 2006

[66] Wright R. The moral animal: Why We Are, the Way We Are: The New Science of Evolutionary Psychology. New York: Vintage Books; 1994

[67] Karp T. What do we really mean by good leadership? Journal of Values-Based Leadership. 2020;**13**(1):1-12

[68] Steinbeck J. The Log From the Sea of Cortez. London: Penguin; 1995

[69] Hobbes T. Leviathan. London: Penguin; 1968

[70] Ridley M. The Origins of Virtue. London: Penguin; 1996

[71] Hessen DO. Vi: Samarbeid-fra celle til samfunn. Oslo: Cappelen Damm; 2017

[72] Kellerman B. The End of Leadership. Brighton: Harvard Business School Press; 2012

[73] Hegel GW. Phänomenologie des Geistes, translated as Phenomenology of Spirit, by Miller AV. Vol. 89. Oxford: Oxford University Press. 1977; p. 64

[74] Collinson DL. Critical leadership studies: Exploring the dialectics of leadership. In: What's Wrong with Leadership? Improving Leadership Research and Practice. New York: Routledge; 2019. pp. 260-278

[75] Parker M. Shut down the business school what's wrong with management education. London Pluto Press; 2018

[76] Illich I. Deschooling Society. London: Pluto Press; 1970

[77] Burns JM. Transforming Leadership. New York: Grove; 2003

[78] Starkey K, Madan P. Bridging the relevance gap: Aligning stakeholders in the future of management research. British Journal of Management [Internet]. 2001;**12**(s1):S3-26. Available from: https://onlinelibrary.wiley.com/doi/abs/10.1111/1467-8551.12.s1.2

[79] Lowe KB, Gardner WL. Ten years of the leadership quarterly. The Leadership Quarterly. 2000;**11**(4):459-514

[80] Gardner WL, Lowe KB, Moss TW, Mahoney KT, Cogliser CC. Scholarly leadership of the study of leadership: A review of The Leadership Quarterly's second decade, 2000-2009. The

Leadership Quarterly. 2010;**21**(6): 922-958

[81] Kaiser RB, Hogan R, Craig SB. Leadership and the fate of organizations. American Psychologist. 2008;**63**(2):96-110

[82] Bryman A. Research methods in the study of leadership. In: Bryman D, editor. The SAGE Handbook of Leadership. London: Sage; 2011. p. 15

[83] Conger JA. The dark side of leadership. Organizational Dynamics. 1990;**19**(2):44-55

[84] Bennis WG, O'Toole J. How business schools have lost their way. Harvard Business Review. 2005;**83**(5):96-104

[85] Ashforth BE. Petty Tyranny in Organizations. Human Relations. 1994;**47**(7):755-778

[86] Elbing C, Elbing AO. Militant Managers. Burr Ridge, IL: Irwin Professional Pub; 1994

[87] Keashly L, Trott V, MacLean LM. Abusive behavior in the workplace: A preliminary investigation. Violence and Victims. 1994;**9**(4):341-357

[88] Vartia M. Bullying at workplaces. In: Towards the 21st Century. Work in the 1990s. Proceedings of an International Symposium on Future Trends in the Changing Working Life, 13-15 August 1991 Proceedings 3, Aavaranta series 29. Lehtinen S, Rantanen J, Juuti P, Koskela A, Lindström K, Rehnström P, Saari J, editors. 131-5, Finnish Institute of Occupational Health, Finnish Employers' Management Development Institute (FEMDI), Helsinki

[89] Bostock WW. Evil, toxic and pathological categories of leadership: Implications for political power. In: Schlegel J, Hansen B, editors. Challenging Evil, Time, Society and Changing Concepts of the Meaning of Evil. Oxford: Inter-Disciplinary Press; 2010. pp. 11-18

[90] Lipman-Blumen J. Toxic leadership: When grand illusions masquerade as noble visions. Leader to Leader. 2005;**2005**(36):29-36

[91] Pelletier KL. Leader toxicity: An empirical investigation of toxic behavior and rhetoric. Leadership. 2010;**6**(4):373-389

[92] Singh N, Sengupta S, Dev S. Toxic leadership: The most menacing form of leadership. Dark sides of Organizational Behavior and Leadership. 2018;**5**:147-164

[93] Schyns B, Schilling J. How bad are the effects of bad leaders? A meta-analysis of destructive leadership and its outcomes. The Leadership Quarterly. 2013;**24**(1):138-158

[94] Shek DTL, Chung P, Dou D. The dark sides of service leaders. In: Brandebo MF, Alvinius A, editors. Dark Sides of Organizational Behaviour and Leadership. London, United Kingdom: Intechopen; 2019. pp. 147-164

[95] Schilling J. From ineffectiveness to destruction: A qualitative study on the meaning of negative leadership. Leadership. 2009;**5**(1):102-128

[96] Gabriel Y, Hirshhorn L. Leaders and followers. In: Gabriel Y, editor. Organizations in Depth: The Psychoanalysis of Organizations. Thousand Oaks: Sage; 2004. pp. 139-165

[97] Tepper BJ. Consequences of abusive supervision. Academy of Management Journal. 2000;**43**(2):178-190

[98] McCall MW, Lombardo MM. Off the Track: Why and How Successful

Executives Get Derailed. Center for Creative Leadership; 1983

[99] Brown ME, Mitchell MS. Ethical and unethical leadership: Exploring new avenues for future research. Greensboro, North Carolina: Business Ethics Quarterly. 2010;**20**(04):583-616

[100] Kets de Vries M, Balazs K. The shadow side of leadership. In: Bryman A, Collinson D, Grint K, Jackson B, Uhl-Bien M, editors. The SAGE Handbook of Leadership. London: SAGE; 2013. pp. 380-392

[101] Bowlby J. Attachment and Loss. New York: Basic Books; 1969

[102] McDougall J. Theaters of the mind. New York: Basic Books; 1985

[103] Winnicott DW. Through paediatrics to psycho-analysis. New York: Basic Books; 1975

[104] Karp T. We are asking the wrong question about leadership: The case for "good-enough" leadership. In: Brandebo MA, Alvinius A, editors. Dark Sides of Organisational Behavior and Leadership. London: IntechOpen; 2018. pp. 47-66

[105] Schyns B, Neves P, Wisse B, Knoll M. Turning a blind eye to destructive leadership: The forgotten destructive leaders. In: What's Wrong with Leadership? New York: Routledge; 2018. pp. 189-206

Chapter 7

Techno-Stress in Organization

Belal Panahi

Abstract

In today's business world, technology is often a strong and influential driver of behavior, causing many challenges and stress to employees' inner and performance, and it causes people's nerves and insides to collapse and even provides conditions where people cannot really get the necessary peace for a long time. In this way, people may be victims of stressful factors that our ancestors only saw in their dreams. This problem, which is introduced as technology stress or techno-stress, arises due to dependence on technology, constant use of technological tools, and fear of lack of necessary technology. In this chapter, techno-stress is introduced and explained. The theoretical foundations of this concept are presented and its dimensions and components are introduced. Also, the consequences of techno-stress are identified and important strategies for managing and controlling its effects are presented.

Keywords: stress, organization, techno-stress, organizational stressors, work roles

1. Introduction

The study of people in work environments has long been the focus of management and behavioral science thinkers, and with the emergence of the field of organizational behavior in the first years of the decade (1960s), more seriousness was done in this matter. Employees of any organization, according to the type of role and mission they have, need to master the cognitive, emotional, and social dimensions to provide quality work according to different job challenges. It should be said that in the job process, due to multiple work pressures, the performance and job satisfaction of employees may be affected [1].

Also, today, information technology is rapidly growing and expanding, and its consequences can have various effects on job performance [2]. Today, employees have access to technologies, such as the internet and office automation, but the amount of use of these tools is often excessive. The use of tools such as e-mail, blogs, the internet, and office automation are very low-cost and accessible methods and can be used to create and share knowledge culture [3]. Thus, we live in an age where technology and the internet play a huge role, and this excessive interaction with technology makes self-regulation difficult. So, if you find yourself glued to your phone or constantly following new technological developments, you may be a victim of technical stress; and this can have a serious impact on our mental health. We live in an age of unlimited technology. People are too focused on technology to disconnect from it, and the pressure to be available is taking a toll on our health.

Although more and more features and apps allow users to control their online time, there is evidence that people cannot escape the pressures of technology. With the increasing use of smartphones and mobile applications, our dependence on technology has also increased significantly.

The use of electronic and computer technologies and systems enables an organization to be more efficient in its core business and more useful in its functional areas. Employees must be able to use these systems or they may be left out. This constant pressure can increase work anxiety. Continuous training of new systems is necessary for many companies. This can cause techno-stress, which itself leads to lower employee performance in terms of job performance. The use of technology can also affect organizational roles. When an organization uses new information systems, it can identify new organizational solutions, which in turn create new roles. Failure of employees to adapt to such changes also causes more tension and stress [4]. With the emergence of techno-stress, organizations must learn how to reduce and manage it. Management can play an important role in the organizational environment and culture of an organization. Management factors have an effect on the level of stress and anxiety of employees.

2. Introducing organizational stressors and techno-stress

Perceived stress is one of the major problems of human society and countless people are involved with it. It seems that stress is a necessary component and an inevitable result of human interaction with the environment. Stress includes physical, mental, and emotional reactions that are experienced as a result of changes and needs in a person's life. These changes can be big or small, and people's responses to life changes are different. Positive stress can be a motivating factor while negative stress can occur when these changes and needs overwhelm the individual. Perceived stress is a psychological state or process during which people perceive their physical and psychological well-being as threatening. In other words, perceived stress is a person's perceived abilities and confidence in facing environmental demands [5]. Events that can cause stress are called stressors. Providing an accurate and clear definition of stress is very difficult because everyone experiences it in a different way and each definition refers to a part of reality. Different theorists have used stress in different ways. One of the common ways of defining stress is to consider it as a stimulus. Holmes and Rahe [6] consider stress as a stimulus that a person needs to adapt to [6]. Therefore, stress, as a stimulus, is any situation that has unusual and extraordinary requests and requires a change in a person's current life pattern [7].

Several definitions related to stress have been provided by experts and experts in psychology and verbology, among which we mention the following:

- Stress is the feeling that a person feels that he/she is out of control.
- Stress is the uncertain human response to pressures.
- Lack of ability between pressures and one's own abilities to deal with it is called stress.
- Stress is a condition or feeling in which a person perceptually believes that the sum of the demands and expectations that exist are beyond the facilities, resources, and capabilities that he/she has.
- Stress is the body's physiological reaction that disturbs the psychological balance in the face of any change, threat, and external or internal pressure.

Some stressful events such as exams, natural disasters, risky jobs, and divorce require a person to perform adaptive behaviors to cope with imposed environmental demands, and since adapting to such events is difficult and potentially dangerous, people get stressed [6]. Today, information technology in organizations is rapidly growing and expanding, which creates numerous jobs in all industrial and service sectors, of course, employment in them requires having the necessary expertise in the field of technology, which raises fears due to insufficient it brings benefits for employees [4].

Generally, stress can come from the environment (situational stress) or from the personal characteristics of a person (mental stress). Situational stress can originate from all issues in our life. At home, at school, and in mutual relationships with other people, we are exposed to a lot of stressors at work. Undoubtedly, all these various sources of stress pile up and add to our overall stress level. This means that the stress caused at home can add to the stress caused by work and vice versa. In the following, various sources of stress are examined.

2.1 Organizational sources of work stress: situational stressors

Most of the stress of the employees comes from the stressful factors of the organizational work environment. Part of this organizational stress comes from the work tasks themselves, such as the physical and psychological needs of performing tasks. Since work organizations are complex social systems in which a person must interact with countless people, organizational stress may arise from work roles. Therefore, various types of work relationships that must be created and implemented for the successful performance of work tasks can lead to stress. These two types of situational stress—task stress and work role stress—can be greatly reduced by management measures.

2.2 Stressors related to work duties

Job overload—A common source of stress is workload-related tasks that occurs when the performance of the task requires more speed, more production, or more concentration. Everyone believes that workload is one of the biggest factors of work stress. The research done on the burden of work shows that this characteristic of work is related to physiological indicators of stress such as increased blood cholesterol and increased heart rate, psychological stress, and finally low quality of work and job satisfaction. In fact, workload has been identified as a common source of stress for various occupations such as office workers, soldiers, air traffic controllers, and healthcare workers. While job overload can cause stress, having less work—below productivity—can also be stressful. Low productivity may occur when a worker feels that his job does not fully utilize all of his knowledge, skills, or abilities, or when the job is boring and monotonous. Some university graduates in low-level positions of administrative work or providing customer service may feel some stress due to the factor of low productivity and lack of use of their knowledge and skills [8].

2.3 Stressors related to work role

2.3.1 Job ambiguity

One of the potential sources of stress caused by the work role is job ambiguity, which occurs when different aspects of a job, such as its duties and requirements, are not clearly defined. Stress occurs when employees are not sure of their responsibilities and duties. Sometimes job ambiguity is referred to as "job uncertainty." This uncertainty is the result of the lack of regular performance feedback that deals with how well or poorly the employees are doing. Research have concluded that supervisors can have a great impact on reducing job uncertainty by clarifying the roles and duties of subordinates. Understanding that job uncertainty has a negative effect on job satisfaction highlights the importance of supervisors' role in reducing uncertainty and stress resulting from it [9].

The conflict between roles can also become a source of the crisis. For example, an employee's work may require long overtime that conflicts with the worker's role in the family as a spouse or guardian. Or if the employee has to perform different roles in his work in such a way that the same issue may lead to stress.

2.3.2 Lack of control

Another important source of work stress is the feeling of lack of control, especially among low-level jobs or in structured organizations. Jobs that are completely limited and dominated by laws, so that workers cannot have any kind of influence on work decisions and the way the work environment works, are probably classified as stressful jobs, especially for those workers who want to be effective in their work. Research have shown that providing a kind of power of control over the work environment in workers through methods such as paying attention to their opinion in the decision-making process or making it possible to adjust their task map, reduces worker stress and increases job satisfaction. On the other hand, there are studies that believe that the feeling of not having control over one's job may not be stressful for many workers, and it may be true that different types of workers are more or less sensitive to having the power to control one's job. In fact, research results have shown that it is the special characteristics of the personality that determine whether a person is stressed or not due to the lack of control over his job.

2.3.3 Physical conditions of work

Physical conditions in the work environment are another organizational resource that leads to worker stress. Jobs that have to be done in high temperatures, loud noises, poor lighting, and poor ventilation can be quite stressful. Dangerous jobs that cause the worker to lose his health, or face the risk of death, or the possibility of amputation are other sources of work stress. Intrapersonal stress—Intrapersonal stress is one of the biggest sources of employee stress that arises from problems caused by interpersonal relationships. Such intrapersonal stress is one of those types of stress that almost every worker will deal with. Intrapersonal stress arises from problems in establishing and maintaining relationships with other people in the workplace. Having a harsh and critical boss with a directive management style will be stressful for any worker. In addition, intrapersonal stress arises when colleagues are in a conflict situation. For example, two employees have to work together when they should be considered for an important position. If both employees have to work together while competing for a position, their work may be extremely stressful for both. There is evidence that organizational policies and power struggles can be an important source of stress caused by the work environment. The inability to get along with other workers, for whatever reason, is another very common source of workplace stress.

2.3.4 Organizational change

Another source of organizational stress is changing. People are usually used to a certain work schedule and a certain work structure and show resistance to change. Most of us want everything to be stable and predictable. Stability in the work environment seems comfortable and reassuring. Therefore, it is not surprising if changes in the work organization cause stress. Some of the common situations of change that lead to labor stress are: company reorganization, merger, counter-merger, or takeover of another company, change in work systems and work technology, change in policy, and change in management or personnel. For example, research results show that physiological responses are stronger in new, unfamiliar, threatening, and challenging situations. Undoubtedly, an event similar to the organization in the company, or merger or takeover, is considered by many experts as a dangerous and stressful thing.

2.3.5 Performance appraisal

Performance appraisal is another source of stress in the organization. There are few people in the organization who want to be evaluated because evaluation is a test of people's competence compared to others and a poor evaluation will have an important effect on a person's job [10].

2.4 Techno-stress

In relation to the activities related to new systems, it refers to the use of technology and new systems that involve the harm caused by the introduction of new technology into the work system [11]. The increasing use of computer systems in the "Information Age" with today's advanced technology has undoubtedly changed many jobs. Many employees, from new employees to high-level managers and executives, spend most of their time in front of computer monitors. The technological revolution has helped to reduce some of the unpleasant aspects of the job. For example, a small number of workers today have to do monotonous or repetitive stressful tasks, because these boring and repetitive tasks are completed by computers. While modern technology has reduced some sources of work stress, it has actually increased other stressors, and maybe even created new stressors. What are the stressors associated with the information age and which workers are likely to be most affected by them?

Technology-related stress has been named "techno-stress." Techno-stress is expressed as stress caused by uncertainty resulting from technological changes. For example, a few decades ago, workers could start a job or learn a trade, and their job did not change significantly during their working period. But today, many workers are faced with jobs that constantly change along with changes in technology. In addition, job uncertainty may be stressful for workers whose work is suddenly computerized or for workers who fear that their work will be jeopardized as their work becomes more computerized.

The research results show that the use of new technology has led to an extraordinary increase in employee stress. Technology-related stress may result from workload or underutilization of skills, lack of control over work, and lack of supervisory support. Such factors are often associated with jobs in which the employee must sit in front of a computer and work with the computer and data for hours on end without having sufficient knowledge, or any knowledge at all, about the final application of the results.

Low-level jobs in the field of information processing produce more stress than jobs such as supervision or professional jobs, due to the same stressful sources caused by technology. There is no doubt that the information age will continue and technological change will be a constant feature of the workplace. As a result, such techno-stress is likely to be permanent. For this reason, creating appropriate methods to help workers who deal with negative stress, will be a very important issue for an organization, regardless of the source of stress.

3. Theoretical foundations, dimensions, and components of techno-stress

3.1 Definition of techno-stress

What is techno-stress? Various definitions have been provided for techno-stress, which include: The stress caused by technology, which is one of the basic problems of today's organizations, is called techno-stress. Techno-stress occurs as a result of dependence on technology or anxiety caused by uncertainty in connection with technology [12]. It is a type of stress caused by rapid changes in technology, resulting in an inability to meet changing competencies. Fatigue and mental stress are caused by the daily use of technology.

- An individual's inability to cope with technology-related demands in the environment. These demands may be considered technical uncertainties, technical insecurity, technical invasiveness, and technical complexity.

- An inability or imbalance resulting from the rapid introduction of new technologies, technological change, or exposure to or overuse of technology that may cause individuals to reject its use.

- A negative psychological response to technology use stems from the perception of a discrepancy between the resources and demands associated with the technology.

- It is a situation where a person has difficulty or inability to learn and use information and communication technologies.

- A condition in which people cannot adapt or cope with new computer technologies in a healthy way.

Techno-stress has been seen in different industries and occupations. The most common of them is in information technology jobs. In this context, businesses always restructure their work processes to appear more active and efficient, especially in the economic field. Even those who work professionally in the field of information technology are not safe from techno-stress. These employees both use technology and suffer from its risks. They learn how to deal with techno-stress by identifying the main roots of stress and applying practical solutions such as necessary training and increasing skills in this field [13].

The large volume of information on the internet has made a classification of information inevitable. Libraries have been struggling with this problem for years. Classifying and categorizing information is a very difficult task, even if we want to use new technologies. Today, some organizations have made it possible for their employees to use new technologies in all their daily work in the workplace. This purposeful and forward-looking way of thinking has made the Berkeley University library one of the most advanced computer libraries. In recent years, many libraries have used this method. Paper catalogs have been replaced by computers that can be easily accessible to users and make it easier to research what they want. Of course, in the meantime, people and library staff have to filter a huge amount of data, which can cause stress [14].

Another industry that is affected by techno-stress is the education industry. In the past years, teachers have experienced a high level of techno-stress due to the continuous use of new technology in schools. Teachers should be able to work with computers without any problems. They should be willing to accept technology in teaching their students. Using PowerPoint and active websites is normal for students in schools. Most students use computers and need to use new educational technology. Teachers who do not want to accept this problem get tired; this increases their techno-stress. Knowing that technology has a great impact on teachers, schools use strategies that can help teachers reduce their techno-stress. This includes more technology training, practice before using technology, changing teaching methods, and teaching how to manage the class [15].

Techno-stress affects an organization from three aspects: organizational, productivity, and health [16]. Technology fatigue causes employees to lose their effectiveness. Managing techno-stress can be difficult for an organization. Researchers examine how organizations deal with techno-stress. They propose methods and solutions based on which it is determined how organizations can manage technology in their organization in order to reduce techno-stress. Also, the identification and management of techno-stress increase the efficiency of the organization. Accordingly, if the level of techno-stress is high, it will be difficult for the organization to access and use technology. Employees of the organization must accept the new technology in order to work with it [16]. According to Researchers, techno-stress can lead to sleep problems and depression. These consequences also affect many other aspects of life such as work and family. The researchers also point out that techno-stress can cause mental and physical problems in employees, which causes inefficiency at work. Also, productivity is one of the main concerns of organizations. By using technology, organizations expect to increase their productivity levels. But if techno-stress also increases as a result of technology, productivity can be affected in various ways [16]. In general, it can be said that three important factors affecting techno-stress include managerial, technological, and personality factors [16].

3.2 Technological factors

Technology factors, such as high volume of technology, technology influx, technology complexity, technology insecurity, and uncertainty, can affect techno-stress. This factor is closely related to techno-stress [4].

3.3 Personality or personal factors

The individual characteristics of the user can affect the level of techno-stress that a person experiences. A person with strong computer skills and experience is likely to experience less techno-stress than someone who is computer literate.

3.4 Management factors

High workload can lead to techno-stress as well as occupational stress. Ambiguity factors in the role, technical support, job security, and work communication can also affect techno-stress. These factors are classified in the management factor category [4].

4. Symptoms and consequences of techno-stress

Techno-stress is considered a new phenomenon in society and organizational culture. Techno-stress is the stress that a person experiences due to dependence on technology or anxiety caused by the uncertainty of communication with technology. This phenomenon reduces the productivity and performance of people in their work. This reduction in productivity lowers the success level of the organization. On the other hand, all types of technology, especially information technology, are changing rapidly, and as a result, organizations that do not update themselves lose the power to compete with other organizations. The use of new technologies can cause stress in employees and thus negatively affect job satisfaction [17].

As mentioned earlier, the term techno-stress refers to a person's inability to cope with technology, which leads to distress. Decades after the development of technology, there is now strong evidence that new technologies have an adverse effect on human health. From computing to data management and the internet, information and communication technologies (ICT) affects every aspect of life in the twenty-first century. The age-old boundaries between work and life blur as we venture into a remote world where it seems almost impossible to disconnect from what's going on around us. How much does technology affect mental health? Do all the emails, social media notifications, and pings on your office messaging systems make you anxious or stressed? Does learning another new software cause you stress? Are the boundaries between home and work life blurred by technology? If so, you may be experiencing a phenomenon known as techno-stress, a term used to describe the negative psychological impact that the use of new technologies can have on us, and how these negative impacts can lead to feelings of anxiety and mental fatigue.

Currently, scientific research on techno-stress shows that the negative psychological relationship with technology mainly manifests itself in two different ways: people's anxiety in understanding and using new technology (technology anxiety), or excessive use of technology (technology addiction).

Techno-stress is different from traditional stress and is caused by technological changes. An individual's inability to disconnect or keep up with the demands of new technology is a growing issue that needs further research. However, important symptoms such as concentration problems, warning signs, and symptoms of techno-stress can cause various physical and mental symptoms. Some people may feel exhausted or depressed. People with techno-stress may feel tension in the body, which can lead to headaches and back pain. Common symptoms and warning signs of techno-stress include poor job performance, feeling ineffective at work, lack of motivation or feelings of indifference, difficulty concentrating, feeling restless or anxious, productivity challenges, posture and muscle tension, insomnia, chronic fatigue, depression disorders, etc., which caused anxiety may cause some people to have stomach pain, nausea, and sleep problems. These symptoms have a great impact on work-life balance and job satisfaction of employees. In general, this stress has various physical, mental, and emotional symptoms that are mentioned in the following:

4.1 Physical symptoms of techno-stress

Headache, sleep disorder, high blood pressure, pain in the neck, back, and shoulder muscles, restlessness, illness, and insomnia.

4.2 Mental symptoms of techno-stress

Many errors in work, problems in concentration, low self-confidence and morale, mental exhaustion, and negative attitude towards the computer.

4.3 Emotional symptoms of techno-stress

Anxiety and fear, helplessness, isolation and despair, irritability, and anger.

4.4 Other problems of techno-stress

Other problems caused by techno-stress include general fatigue, not having enough time for sustained thinking, less opportunity for the creative problem-solving, lack of balance between work and personal life, and reduced job satisfaction. Finally, it can be said that the problems caused by techno-stress take away the pleasure of a good life from people and it should be managed seriously.

5. Managing and controlling techno-stress

With the emergence of techno-stress, organizations must learn how to reduce or manage it. Organizations have been struggling with this problem for years. Especially working with information is very hard and difficult work that increases the amount of techno-stress [18].

Therefore, new technologies are constantly changing and businesses must use technologies to improve and progress. Applying new technologies in a way that is compatible with the activities of the organization is a very difficult task. An organization should analyze its solutions and choose the best and most useful way to use technology. In today's global markets, businesses are constantly looking for competitive solutions to overcome their competitors. Human resource systems and customer relationship management systems have been created to increase productivity and efficiency. If new technologies are not used, the possibility of new organizational issues may arise among the employees of that organization. Depending on how an employee approaches technology, using technology can cause tension and anxiety. The use of software or hardware may cause dissatisfaction and have a negative effect on the efficiency of an employee [19]. Preventing or minimizing the negative effects of techno-stress may seem impossible and very difficult at first, but it can be managed with the following techniques:

1. Determining a time to rest Install an application or programs on your computer to tell you the time. Then, use that to schedule rest times for yourself and stick to it.

2. Determining a specific time to search in social networks if you must visit social networks every day, and turn off notifications and ads on your phone. You can even delete apps you do not use.

3. Turn off personal digital tools while working Turn off all your digital devices while working, relaxing, and sleeping so you do not lose your peace of mind due to timely and timeless messages.

4. Reducing unnecessary communications filter non-essential messages on your cell phone and set a specific time of day to answer other messages.

5. Writing on paper if you feel that turning on the computer to type a text makes you distracted and immersed in searching on the computer or the Internet, write your content on paper if possible. In this way, you will stay away from technology as before.

6. Learning technology if you have to use digital tools and have to learn to work with modern technologies, learn them in training classes so that you donot get anxiety and worry caused by technology.

7. Self-awareness and preventing drowning while using technology. The first step in dealing with this type of reaction is awareness. If we become more aware of our behavior in social networks, there is a greater possibility that we can separate the harmful effects from beneficial effects and avoid using it in a harmful way. Therefore, every time you experience techno-stress from a social network, it might be better to put your device away.

8. Preventing multitasking and preventing doing several tasks at the same time part of the reason for techno-stress is that technology has enabled us to be very efficient and productive. Because technology promotes doing multi-stage activities or "multi-tasking," people are forced to engage their minds and body in several tasks at the same time; for example, driving and talking on their cell phones at the same time, or sending text messages while driving or crossing intersections. However, such people who multitask at the same time are actually less productive than those who focus on one task. Additionally, there is clear evidence that "multitasking" (doing several things at the same time) leads to driving accidents and other harmful consequences such as short-term memory loss. What is not so clear is what happens to someone who is constantly using technological tools.

9. Doing sports. Unfortunately, the existence of stress and anxiety in today's organizations is an important fact. A fact that can have a negative impact on the quality of life of the organization's employees. Certainly, people may experience this feeling at any time; but the most important thing is to find suitable ways of exercise to reduce stress and anxiety and manage it. Exercise is one of the most available and best ways to reduce and manage all types of stress. Almost any form of exercise, from aerobics to yoga, can be a major factor in reducing anxiety and stress. It is not necessary for people to be professional athletes, but people can remove tension and mental anxiety by using the simplest sports exercises even at home and to manage them. Doing sports is a powerful natural anti-depressant and anxiety reliever that relieves stress. In general, exercise will have many benefits on physical and mental health and stress relief [20].

10. Expecting technological developments and changes. Change and improvement are in the nature of technology. No matter how comfortable you are with your

current computer, mobile phone, or pocket computer! Sometimes you will need to upgrade to a newer version.

11. Using digital tools at designated times or turning them off completely if possible. Today, each of the users of digital tools, whether adults or teenagers, and even children, spend hours working or spending time with it daily without knowing the principles of ergonomics, and unfortunately, these hours are also increasing. Naturally, it is not surprising to see the spread of physical and mental problems caused by not following the principles of working with mobile phones. Prolonged use of mobile phones during the day causes serious damage to wrists, fingers, spine, neck, shoulders, and eyes. In general, the World Health Organization has pointed out the negative impact of all electronic devices and not only smartphones on the human body, and according to this organization, they increase the possibility of contracting cancer. Among the time management tools, we can mention tools such as calendar, note-taking software, time tracker, specialized management programs, etc. Using these tools is amazing for better time management. Because they increase our productivity and make it easier for us to revise our work and create more useful habits. To choose the time management tools is different according to the needs and goals of the audience. For example, some people like to use digital tools for time management, but others prefer to use written and manual tools. Due to the wide range of these tools, some of them have attracted the attention of more audiences due to their ease of use and facilities.

Author details

Belal Panahi
Department of Management, Payame Noor University (PNU), Tehran, Iran

*Address all correspondence to: panahi1980@yahoo.com

References

[1] ParsaiKia F, Rezaian A. Examining the relationship between organizational support and organizational commitment and intention to leave institute in a government organization. Quarterly of Health Management. 2011;**35**:56-43

[2] Zolfaqari M. The Relationship between Techno-Stress and Job Burnout with Job Satisfaction of Municipal Employees in Isfahan City. Khorasgan: Khorasgan Islamic Azad University; 2012

[3] Mar H. Relationship of techno-stress with job burnout and job satisfaction of employees. Behavior and Human Decision Processes. 2014;**86**(2):278-321

[4] Moridzadeh A. Investigating the Role of Technology in the Workplace and Perceived Organizational Support on Employee Job Satisfaction. Marvdasht: Marvdasht Islamic Azad University; 2012

[5] Clark A. Stress, Appraisal and Coping. NewYork: Springe; 2010. pp. 127-138

[6] Holmes TH, Rahe RH. The social readjustment rating scale. Journal of Psychosomatic Research. 1967;**11**(2):213-218

[7] SajadManesh M. The Relationship between Organizational Health and Job Attachment and Stress among National Ahvaz Drilling Workers. Ahvaz: Ahvaz Islamic Azad University; 2011

[8] Mehdad A. Employee Psychology. Isfahan: Jungle; 2011

[9] Saatchi M. Industrial and Organizational Psychology. Tehran: Virayesh Ed; 2006

[10] Saatchi M. Applied Psychology for Managers. Tehran: Virayesh Ed; 2011

[11] Dividsoon T. Relationship between of technology organizational culture social with job satisfaction. The Journal of the Academy of Management. 2013;**56**(1):396-406

[12] Khordmand R, Nazim M. Investigating the relationship between technology and job satisfaction of employees. Journal of Thought and Behavior. 2010;**11**(2):42-31

[13] Scats F. The model job satisfaction. Journal of Social Behavior. 2015;**32**: 323-334

[14] Quchani S, Badrizadeh S. The effect of techno-stress on establishing job satisfaction. Research in Industry. 2011;**7**(26):1-10

[15] Rostami S. The Relationship between Organizational Climate and Desire to Stay in the Job with Job Satisfaction of Shahrekord Librarians. Karaj: Karaj Islamic Azad University; 2014

[16] Ezadi M, Hosseinian Nejad S, Sargazai S, Shoja Nia S, gerae-Shahri, N. The effect of managerial factors on technostress in the organization. Management Transformation Quarterly. 2014;**5**(17):90-75

[17] Lazaro S, Capones H, Antonett H. Relationship of techno stress with satisfaction job. Journal of Personality and Social Psychology. 2015;**32**:323-334

[18] Debl JC, Anderson CA. Relationship between of stay on job with job satisfaction. Journal of IO Psychology. 2014;**40**:757-768

[19] Entezari A. Investigating the Relationship between Technology and Providing Information with the Job

Satisfaction of Shiraz Librarians. Ahvaz: Ahvaz Islamic Azad University; 2011

[20] Fathizadeh M, Alimoradi S. The effect of aerobic exercise on the level of depression, anxiety and stress of women with hypothyroidism under clinical conditions. Nursing and Midwifery Journal. 2018;**17**(9):749-757

Chapter 8

Negative Aspects of Teacher Burnout Problem on Educational Organization

Huijeong Oh

Abstract

Teachers are prone to burnout problems due to the nature of their jobs. Teacher burnout is a very serious educational problem in the field of education, and the problem is gradually getting worse. The problem of teacher burnout negatively affects not only the individual teachers but also the overall educational organization. Teacher burnout has a negative correlation with teacher efficacy, teacher enthusiasm, and job satisfaction. These negatively affect classes, school climate, and school culture. In addition, the problem of teacher burnout may lead to the disintegration of the school organization by increasing teachers' departure from teaching. Thus, the teacher burnout problem acts as a hindrance to the effective functioning of the school organization. Ultimately, it has negative consequences for the achievement of educational goals. Therefore, in order to lead an effective school organization, it is necessary to systematically diagnose the problem of teacher burnout, management, and measures are needed to improve it.

Keywords: teacher burnout, educational organization, educational organization effectiveness, class, school climate, school culture

1. Introduction

In modern society, people who experience chronic occupational stress while experiencing new lifestyles, rapid changes in human relationships, and various daily events in a complex organizational society are physically and psychologically in trouble with so-called burnout, a phenomenon of mental exhaustion [1–4]. This kind of burnout problem is a big topic in the educational field and educational organizations [5–7].

As teachers are representative assistant professionals, the problem of burnout is more prominent among teachers, some even evaluate the teacher organization as the organization that will be the most exhausted. Such teacher burnout is a very serious educational problem. As concerned, as the problem of teacher burnout is becoming increasingly serious in the recent education field, as a result, the number of teachers leaving the teaching profession is rapidly increasing. These pathological phenomena suggest that the burnout problem experienced by teachers has reached a fairly high level, and if it is not adequately resolved, it can negatively affect not only individual teachers but also the entire educational organization.

In previous studies, teacher burnout had a negative impact on job enthusiasm or school educational performance or acted as a factor preventing teachers from engaging in organizational citizenship behavior such as altruistic behavior. It also had an effect on individual teachers, such as leaving the teaching profession, job satisfaction, and reduced efficacy. In addition, it has a negative impact on students' adaptation and academic self-efficacy, as well as reducing teachers' emotional immersion in educational activities, which can negatively affect teachers' emotional and subjective well-being [8–13]. Burnout teachers find it difficult to devote themselves to school work, become negligent in service, and find it difficult to empathize with student guidance and character guidance. They act mechanically in their relationships with students, parents, and administrators, lose creativity and initiative in their work, and lose interest in caring for students and guiding subjects [14]. It shows that teacher burnout causes various dysfunctions not only to individual teachers but also to school organizations and students, making it difficult to expect successful education from burnout teachers [12].

As such, teacher burnout has a negative correlation with teacher efficacy, teacher enthusiasm, and job satisfaction, which negatively affects classes, school climate, and school culture. In addition, the problem of teacher burnout may lead to disintegration of school organizations by increasing teachers' departure from the teaching profession. Thus, the problem of teacher burnout acts as a hindrance to the effective functioning of school organizations, ultimately causing negative results in achieving educational goals. Therefore, in order to lead an effective school organization, it is necessary to systematically diagnose and manage the problem of teacher burnout, and prepare measures to improve it. Therefore, in this chapter, we will identify the problem of teacher burnout, ascertain how it affects educational organizations in schools based on empirical research results, and propose measures to solve the problem of teacher burnout.

2. The problem of teacher burnout in the education field

Burnout can be defined as a phenomenon of physical and mental exhaustion caused by negative consequences in physiological and behavioral aspects due to excessive job stress [1, 2]. The main symptoms of this burnout include depersonalization, emotional exhaustion, and a diminished sense of personal fulfillment [15]. Burnout is common in helping professions such as health care, education, and social work that maintain and help people in close relationships over a long period of time [1, 16].

As teachers are the representative helping professions, the problem of burnout appears more prominently among teachers [17], and someone evaluated the teacher group as the group most likely to be burnt out [18]. In addition, teacher burnout was viewed as the most serious educational problem [17]. The reasons are that teachers, as the subject of education, have a huge impact on the overall education, determine the quality of education, and are the most important condition that determines the success or failure of education. After all, when a teacher burns out, it can have a negative impact on education as a whole.

According to previous studies, it is reported that approximately 1/3 of teachers experience job stress [5], and the stress caused by external or human factors that persists chronically in the educational field causes psychological burnout in teachers [5, 17].

In addition, it requires teachers to continuously perform various roles such as subject guidance, life guidance, character guidance, safety guidance, and other administrative tasks in the recent education field [19]. Accordingly, the stress and psychological burden experienced by teachers are increasing. As a case in point, there is a survey result conducted in Korea, which has a world-class passion for education and excellent human resources as teachers. In a survey of 1674 teachers, 96.5% responded that they did emotional labor, and 78.1% of them suffered from severe burnout due to stress such as depression, anger, and loss of self-esteem. In the end, this problem of teacher burnout has a negative impact on educational activities (91.6%), and the case of seriously considering retirement was also very high at 72.2% [20].

As such, the problem of teacher burnout is becoming increasingly serious in the educational field and educational organizations, and the phenomenon of teacher resignation is rapidly increasing as a result. As teachers are exposed to long-term stress, their physical, emotional, and mental energy is depleted and they face the problem of burnout. Such burnout has a negative impact on teachers' overall work, including teaching activities, and on educational organizations such as fellow teachers and students [2]. Accordingly, it is necessary to clearly identify and manage the problem of teacher burnout in the educational field.

3. Negative aspects of teacher burnout problem on educational organization

In this section, we will examine the negative aspects of teacher burnout in the educational field that affect educational organizations. The negative effects of teacher burnout will be examined in terms of the individual and organizational aspects of teachers.

3.1 Teacher burnout, teacher efficacy, teacher enthusiasm, and satisfaction with the teaching profession

Teacher burnout is the physical and mental depletion of teachers themselves, which leads to various pathological phenomena. In particular, the proportion of psychological pathology caused by intellectual work or emotional labor performed by teachers in educational organizations is high. Also, psychological pathology can cause physical pathology and has a great adverse effect on teachers' lives. Accordingly, the negative impact of teacher burnout on the personal, psychological, and emotional aspects of teachers is examined in terms of teacher efficacy, teacher enthusiasm, and satisfaction with the teaching profession as follows.

First, it was found that teacher burnout and teacher efficacy had a negative correlation, and teacher burnout had a negative effect on teacher efficacy [21–24]. Teacher efficacy is an application of Bandura's self-efficacy theory to teachers and refers to teachers' own beliefs and perceptions of how much positive influence a teacher can have on learners' learning [25, 26]. Teacher efficacy is like the belief in oneself that a teacher can contribute to raising the level of achievement of learners by guiding learners to set high goals and continuously strive to achieve them [23]. As such, teacher efficacy is a strong indicator of teaching effectiveness [27] and is recognized as the variable that has the most consistent and lasting effect on learner achievement among various teachers' inner beliefs or attitudes that affect their teaching behavior [28]. In addition, it is reported that teacher efficacy affects various areas including teacher's passion, persistence, responsibility, and teaching behavior [29]. Therefore, the fact that teacher burnout has a negative effect on teacher efficacy suggests that it can negatively affect teachers' passion, persistence, responsibility, teaching behavior and teaching effects, and even learners' achievements.

Second, it was found that teacher burnout and teacher enthusiasm also had a negative correlation, and teacher burnout had a negative effect on teacher enthusiasm [22, 30]. Teacher enthusiasm is defined as a positive and satisfying state of mind associated with teachers and consists of three motivating constructs: vigor, dedication, and absorption [31]. Vigor is mental cheerfulness and resilience while working, a high level of energy and willingness to put forth effort in one's work, and perseverance in the face of difficulties. Dedication means the importance, enthusiasm, inspiration, pride, and challenge of the work. Absorption refers to a state of complete concentration on one's work, a state of immersion, and a state in which it is difficult to think separately from work [30, 31]. The higher the teacher burnout, the lower the vigor, dedication, and absorption, and the lower the teacher enthusiasm, leading to dehumanization and a decrease in personal achievement, negatively affecting organizational commitment [7, 30].

Third, it was found that teacher burnout and satisfaction with teaching profession also had a negative correlation, and teacher burnout had a negative effect on satisfaction with teaching profession [2, 22]. Satisfaction with the teaching profession is the degree to which one demonstrates one's expertise and satisfies one's personal needs in the process of performing one's role as a teacher. Also, it refers to a psychological state that includes emotions that are determined by the level at which the individual teacher's needs are judged to be actually met through teaching experience [32, 33]. In addition, it is defined as an attitude or mindset in which a teacher actively and voluntarily participates in teaching through psychological, social, and economic satisfaction as a member of an organization and contributes to the achievement of the organization's goals [34]. Satisfaction with the teaching profession can lead to organizational performance through the effect of increasing productivity, can maintain good interpersonal relationships within the organization, and can reduce turnover and absenteeism rates. Therefore, due to the negative effect of teacher burnout on satisfaction with teaching profession, those with high burnout were more likely to be absent or tardy in the organization than those with low burnout, and their performance was significantly lower, resulting in a higher retirement rate [17].

As such, teacher burnout has an adverse effect on teacher efficacy, teacher enthusiasm, and satisfaction with teaching profession, which negatively affects not only individual teachers but also educational organizations such as teaching effectiveness, learner achievement, organizational commitment, organizational performance decrease, and organizational dropout.

3.2 Teacher burnout problem, class, school climate, and school culture

As mentioned earlier, the problem of teacher burnout affects the entire life of teachers, and burnout teachers have difficulty fulfilling their role as teachers in educational organizations, which has negative consequences in various areas of educational organizations. Therefore, the negative impact of teacher burnout on the organizational aspect will be examined in terms of classes, school climate, and school culture.

First, the problem of teacher burnout has a negative correlation with the class, and it was found that the problem of teacher burnout has a negative effect on the class [21, 35, 36]. Teacher burnout reduces the ability to perform tasks and work with learners, resulting in a decrease in the quality of teaching activities. In addition, burnout teachers lose interest and enthusiasm in subject instruction, put less effort into teaching, avoid contact with students, do not accept advice from others, and are more likely to lose patience [35]. Also, the peculiarity is that the problem of teacher burnout can have a negative impact on teaching by partially mediating teacher efficacy [21]. Teacher burnout can have a direct negative impact on class, but it can also have an indirect negative impact on class by lowering teacher efficacy. In addition, since the negative impact of teacher burnout on teaching is greater than the negative impact of teacher burnout on teacher efficacy, it is necessary to pay attention to the fact that the negative aspect of teacher burnout on educational organizations may be greater.

Second, it was found that the problem of teacher burnout has a negative correlation with the school climate and school culture, and that the problem of teacher burnout has a negative impact on the school climate and school culture [22, 37–39]. School climate is the personality of a school organization that has a different feeling or uniqueness for each school [40] and means the norms and expectations shared by school members [41]. School climate is an internal characteristic that distinguishes one school from another and influences the behavior of school members. Therefore, it can be said to be the enduring quality of the school environment as perceived by members of school behavior [34]. Meanwhile, culture is a general term for the values, norms, beliefs, etc. that community members generally share. It affects the behaviors of members and the social system and plays a role in organically connecting and adjusting them [42, 43]. In general, culture can be said to be a greater concept that encompasses climate. The school organization also has its own unique culture, and the school culture is very influential and important in the school field, as compared to the lens through which members of the school organization view themselves and the world [44]. Teacher burnout is highly contagious and, along with various physical behaviors, permeates and negatively affects the school climate and school culture, just as one individual's frustration can affect others and burn out the entire school organization [38]. In addition, negative school climate and school culture are shown to deepen teacher burnout, so it is necessary to pay attention to their interactive influence relationship.

As such, it can be confirmed that the problem of teacher burnout has a negative relationship with the teaching field, which is the core area of educational organization, and the climate and culture that affects the overall educational organization and has a negative impact on educational organization.

4. Measures to solve the problem of teacher burnout

The problem of teacher burnout is a factor that adversely affects the lives of individual teachers and the overall educational organization, and it is necessary to solve it in order to increase the effectiveness of teachers and educational organizations. Therefore, it is necessary to diagnose the problem of teacher burnout and prepare policies to manage and improve it. Since teacher burnout reduces teacher efficacy, teacher enthusiasm, and satisfaction with the teaching profession, and it has a negative impact on classes and school climate and culture, special attention should be paid to solving the problem of teacher burnout in the promotion of education policies that strengthen the improvement of class-centered school culture. In terms of education policy, the measures are presented as follows.

Through the vitalization of voluntary professional learning communities in schools, the professionalism of teachers and the cooperative teacher community are strengthened, and by utilizing this, a culture of communication and collaboration within the teacher community about the problem of teacher burnout is created. In addition, in providing teacher-tailored support through the operation of a supervision support group at the level of local offices of education, it is necessary to consider matters related to teacher burnout. For example, when forming a consulting support group, it will be effective if psychology and counseling experts are placed together. This is because it is necessary to properly manage and heal the psychological problems of teachers as it was confirmed in this study that the problem of teacher burnout of emotional exhaustion and dehumanization exists in the school field and that teacher burnout has a negative effect on the educational organization. In addition, among the educational policies that can be implemented at the level of local offices of education, there are activations such as expanding support for class and evaluation and devising plans to reduce administrative work for teachers. Through this, it is possible to reduce the workload of teachers, thereby contributing to solving the burnout problem that may occur due to excessive work. In addition, it is necessary to establish policies related to the health of school organizations and to expand and apply them so that all members of school organizations can participate. Developing customized training for each stage of the teaching career, it helps to solve problems commonly faced by teachers at each stage of the teaching career. Also, it is necessary to solve the burnout problem resulting from the relationship between educational communities through life education that respects and considers each other and improves sensitivity to human rights [5, 17]. Furthermore, it is proposed to organize a related department or organization that systematically diagnoses and manages the problem of teacher burnout, prepares improvement measures, and actively implements that.

5. Conclusions

This study examined the negative aspects of teacher burnout on educational organizations in the education field. Teacher burnout reduces teacher efficacy, teacher enthusiasm, and satisfaction with the teaching profession, and negatively affects classes, school climate, and school culture. Also, there is a high possibility that the negative aspects appearing throughout the educational organization will intensify according to the chain phenomenon in which each variable negatively affected by teacher burnout has another negative impact on the educational organization. In addition, as the problem of teacher burnout is gradually becoming more serious in the school field, the problem of deteriorating the effectiveness of educational organizations due to the problem of teacher burnout will gradually appear at a serious level.

Accordingly, efforts are required in terms of educational organizations to diagnose the problem of teacher burnout, manage it systematically, and improve it. Provide prevention and treatment support for teacher burnout, creation of a culture of communication and cooperation within educational organizations, enhancement of welfare benefits for teachers and educational organizations, and support for professional development. Through this, it is possible to solve the problem of teacher burnout and increase the effectiveness of the educational organization so that it can ultimately achieve the educational goal.

DOI: http://dx.doi.org/10.5772/intechopen.1001062

Conflict of interest

This chapter was written based on a review of the study "Analysis of the Effect of Teacher Burnout Problem on Class Through Teacher Efficacy" conducted by the author in 2021.

Thanks

My beloved family, thank you always.

Author details

Huijeong Oh
Gongju National University of Education, The Center for Global Teacher Education, Gongju, Republic of Korea

*Address all correspondence to: dna1g@icloud.com

References

[1] Freudenberger H. The staff burnout syndrome in alternative institutions. Psychotherapy. 1974;**12**(1):73-82. DOI: 10.1037/h0086411

[2] Maslach C. Burned-out. Human Behavior. 1976;**9**(5):16-22

[3] Paykel E. Life events and depression: A controlled study. Archives of General Psychiatry. 1969;**21**(6):753-760. DOI: 10.1001/archpsyc.1969.01740240113014

[4] Thoits P. Multiple identities: Examining gender and marital status differences in distress. American Sociological Review. 1986;**51**(2):259-272. DOI: 10.2307/2095520

[5] Betoret F. Stressors: Self-efficacy, coping resources, and burnout among secondary school teachers in Spain. Educational Psychology. 2006;**26**(4):519-539. DOI: 10.1080/01443410500342492

[6] Betoret F. Self-efficacy, school resources, job stress and burnout among Spanish primary and secondary school teachers: A structural equation approach. Educational Psychology. 2009;**29**(1):45-68. DOI: 10.1080/01443410802459234

[7] Hakanen J, Bakker A, Schaufeli W. Burnout and work engagement among teachers. Journal of School Psychology. 2006;**43**(6):495-513. DOI: 10.1016/j.jsp.2005.11.001

[8] Kang W. The study of quitting a teaching profession caused by occupational stress and emotional burnout in special education teachers. Emotional Disturbances & Learning Disabilities. 1997;**13**(2):45-67

[9] Lee J. The influence of teacher's professional perception and job stress on the teaching efficacy at child care centers for special children. Korean Journal of Early Childhood Special Education. 2010;**10**(4):115-133

[10] Lee J. The relationship of teacher's burnout and subjective well-being with organizational commitment as a mediator. The Journal of Korean Teacher Education. 2010;**27**(3):143-164. DOI: 10.24211/tjkte.2010.27.3.143

[11] Lee J. The analysis of effects between job-satisfaction, burnout and perceived teacher's emotional intelligence in early childhood teaching. The Korean Journal Child Education. 2007;**16**(4):199-210

[12] Han K. An exploratory study on the relationships among teacher's social support and burnout and organizational citizenship behavior. Korean Journal of Human Resources Development. 2004;**6**(2):45-70

[13] Woolfolk A, Rosoff B, Hoy W. Teachers' sense of efficacy and their beliefs about managing students. Teaching and Teacher Education. 1990;**6**(2):137-148. DOI: 10.1016/0742-051X(90)90031-Y

[14] Kim J, Kim T. Teachers' Job Stress and Burnout. Seoul: Pakhaksa; 2006

[15] Maslach C, Jackson S. The measurement of experience burnout. Journal of Occupational Behavior. 1981;**2**(2):99-113. DOI: 10.1002/job.4030020205

[16] Mechteld R, Visser E, Smets F, Oort C. Stress, satisfaction and bumout among dutch medical specialists. Canadian Medical Association Journal. 2003;**168**(3):271-275

[17] Faber B. Stress and burnout in suburban teachers. The Journal of

Education Research. 1984;**77**(6):325-331. DOI: 10.1080/00220671.1984.10885550

[18] Shaw S, Bensky J, Dixon B, Bonneau R. Burnout among special educators: Cause and coping strategies. In: Proceedings of the Ninth Annual Invitation Conference on Leadership in Special Education Program. Minneapolis; 1981

[19] Oh H, Kim K. Social expectations of teacher's roles: Trend research on teacher's role expectations with content analysis of the newspaper articles from 2007 to 2016. The Journal of Korean Teacher Education. 2017;**34**(3):139-166. DOI: 10.24211/tjkte.2017.34.3.139

[20] Korea Education Newspaper. Faculty Members Who Want to Leave Hurt... Classrooms are Hurting too. [Internet]. 2014 http://www.hangyo.com/app/news/article_print.asp?idx=43418 [Accessed: February 29, 2020]

[21] Oh H. Analysis of the effect of teacher burnout problem on class through teacher efficacy. The Journal of Korean Teacher Education. 2021;**38**(1):273-292. DOI: 10.24211/tjkte.2021.38.1.273

[22] Oh H. Analysis of the influence of school's democratic decision-making authority on teacher efficacy, enthusiasm, satisfaction, and burnout through school climate. In: Proceedings of the 2022 Busan Eudcation Longitudinal Study Conference. Busan; 2022

[23] Schwarzer R, Hallum S. Perceived teacher self-efficacy as a predictor of job stress and burnout: Mediation analyses. Applied Psychology. 2008;**57**(1):152-171. DOI: 10.1111/j.1464-0597.2008.00359.x

[24] Skaalvik E, Skaalvik S. Teacher self-efficacy and teacher burn out: A study of relations. Teaching and Teacher Education. 2010;**26**(4):1059-1069. DOI: 10.1016/j.tate.2009.11.001

[25] Ashton P. Motivation and the teachers' sense of efficacy. In: Ames C, Ames R, editors. Research on Motivation in Education. Vol. 2. The Classroom Milieu. Cambridge, Massachusetts, United States: Academic Press; 1985. pp. 141-171

[26] Bandura A. Self-efficacy: Toward a unifying theory of behavioral change. Psychological Review. 1977;**84**(2):191-215. DOI: 10.1037/0033-295X.84.2.191

[27] Bandura A. Self-efficacy. Harvard Mental Health Letter. 1997;**13**(9):4-6

[28] Ashton P. Teacher efficacy: A motivational paradigm for effective teacher education. Journal of Teacher Education. 1984;**35**(5):287-232. DOI: 10.1177/002248718403500507

[29] Tschannen-Moran M, Hoy A, Hoy W. Teacher efficacy: Its meaning and measure. Review of Educational Research. 1998;**68**(2):202-248. DOI: 10.3102/00346543068002202

[30] Schaufeli W, Bakker A. Job demands, job resources and their relationship with burnout and engagement: A multi-sample study. Journal of Organizational Behavior. 2004;**25**(3):293-315. DOI: 10.1002/job.248

[31] Schaufeli W, Salanova M, Gonzalez-Roma V, Bakker A. The measurement of engagement and burnout: A two sample confirmatory factor analytic approach. Journal of Happiness Studies. 2002;**3**(1):71-92. DOI: 10.1023/A:1015630930326

[32] Evans L. Understanding teacher morale and job satisfaction. Teaching and Teacher Education: An International Journal of Research and Study. 1997;**13**(8):831-845. DOI: 10.1016/S0742-051X(97)00027-9

[33] Gorton R, Schneider G. School-Based Leadership: Challenges and

Opportunities. Dubuque: Wim. C. Brown Company Publisher; 1991

[34] Hoy W, Miskel C. Educational Administration: Theory, Research & Practice. 6th ed. New York: McGraw-Hill; 2001

[35] Schwab R, Jackson S, Schuler R. Educator burnout: Sources and consequences. Educational Research Quarterly. 1986;**10**(3):14-30

[36] Tschannen-Moran M, Hoy A. Teacher efficacy: Capturing an elusive construct. Teaching and Teacher Education. 2001;**17**(7):783-805. DOI: 10.1016/S0742-051X(01)00036-1

[37] Bitsadze M, Japaridze M. Personal and social aspects of teacher burnout in Georgia. Problems of Education in the 21th Century. 2014;**59**(1):7-14. DOI: 10.33225/pec/14.59.07

[38] Cherniss C. Professional Burnout in Human Service Organization. New York: Praeger Publishers; 1980

[39] Grayson J, Alvarez H. School climate factors relating to teacher burnout: A mediator model. Teaching and Teacher Education. 2008;**24**(5):1349-1363. DOI: 10.1016/j.tate.2007.06.005

[40] Halpin A, Croft D. The Organizational Climate of Schools. Chicago: Midwest Administration Center of the University of Chicago; 1963

[41] Brookover W, Schweitzer J, Schneider J, Beady C, Flood P, Wisenbaker J. Elementary school social climate and school achievement. American Educational Research Journal. 1978;**15**(2):301-318. DOI: 10.2307/1162468

[42] Owens R. Organizational Behavior in Education. Boston: Allyn and Bacon; 1995

[43] Schein E. Oraganizational Culture and Leadership. San Francisco: Jossey-Bass; 2004

[44] Deal T, Kennedy A. Corporate Culture: The Rites and Rituals of Corporate Life. Boston: Addison-Wesley; 1982